I KNOW I AM RUDE

PRINCE PHILIP'S LIFE
IN HIS OWN WORDS

Nigel Cawthorne

GIBSON SQUARE

This edition first published in 2021 by Gibson Square in the UK

info@gibsonsquare.com
www.gibsonsquare.com
ISBN   9781783342198

Contents

Philip on Philip

Although Prince Philip published a number of books, he never planned to write an autobiography. 'I don't spend a lot of time looking back,' he said in an interview on his ninetieth birthday. He would have another seven years before retiring from public life in 2017 to change his mind, but he never did. Consequently, we must build a portrait of him from what he says about himself. 'I know I am rude,' he once wrote. 'But it's fun.'

His forthright manner arrived early. At the age of twenty-one, he wrote to a relative whose son had just been killed in the war, saying: 'I know you will never think much of me. I am rude and unmannerly and I say many things out of turn which I realise afterwards must have hurt someone. Then I am filled with remorse and I try to put matters right.'

When asked if this trait was due to his turbulent childhood being passed around family members, he drily replied: 'Wherever I happened to be. It was no great deal I just lived my life.' 'I haven't been trying to psychoanalyse myself all the time.' 'But some people might...' his interviewer interjected. 'Well, some people might,' he countered. 'I'm telling you what I felt.' After all, he said later: 'What's there to complain about?' These things happen.'

One of the duke's biographers asked him how he thought he was seen. 'I don't know,' he said. 'A refugee husband, I suppose.' 'If anything, I've thought of myself as Scandinavian. Particularly, Danish,' he told the *Independent* in 1992. Although he was born on the island of Corfu in Greece, he was both a Prince of Greece and Denmark.

In 1947, he changed his surname from Schleswig-Holstein-Sonderburg-Glücksburg to Mountbatten, the name adopted by his mother's family, Battenberg, during the First World War. 'We spoke English at home,' Prince Philip said, his mother's native language. 'The others learned Greek,' he said. 'I could understand a certain amount of it. But then the conversation would go into French. Then it went into German, on occasion, because we had German cousins. If you couldn't think of a word in one language, you tended to go off in another.' Just how tenuous he felt his position to be was witnessed by what he wrote in a visitor's book in 1946: 'Whither the storm carries me, I go a willing guest.'

Even marriage to the heir to the British throne did not give him the security he craved. When the Queen came to the throne in 1952, he wanted the dynasty to be called the House of Mountbatten, but the Queen took the advice of Prime Minister Winston Churchill and kept the dynasty name Windsor which the royal family had taken since dropping the Germanic surname Saxe-Coburg-Gotha in World War I. Philip complained to a friend: 'I'm nothing but a bloody amoeba. I am the only man in the country not allowed to give his name to his children.' He once remarked: 'Constitutionally, I don't exist.'

The worst of its part of marrying British royalty was having to give up his career in the Navy. 'If I thought of it at all,' he said, 'it was that I thought I could perfectly go on with my career. It would have been of great value to the Queen to have someone who was, in a sense, professionally qualified in something, not just traipsing around,' he said.

When asked how difficult it was to give up his career in the Navy, he said replied: 'Well, how long is a piece of string?' He found himself thrown in at the deep end and swamped with royal duties. On leaving the Navy and taking on royal duties: 'The first ten years I don't remember much about.'

But he had no choice. On another occasion he explained the necessity of giving up his dream: 'In 1947 I thought I was going to have a career in the Navy, but it became obvious there was no hope. The Royal Family then was just the King and the Queen and the two Princesses. The only other male member was the Duke of Gloucester. There was no choice. It just happened. You have to make compromises. That's life. I accept it. I tried to make the best of it.'

He rued the loss of a naval career, but keeps a practical perspective: 'There was no question of my going back, I had to do that but at that time I had not thought that was going to be the end of a sort of naval career. That sort of crept up on me and it became more and more obvious that I could not go back to it,' he said. 'But it's no good regretting things – it simply did not happen and I have been doing other things instead.'

He had fond memories of the sea. 'The sea is an extraordinary master or mistress,' he said: 'It has such extraordinary moods that sometimes you feel this is the only sort of life – and ten minutes later you're praying for death.'

His decision to join the Royal Navy in 1940 he has explained light-heartedly and truthfully: 'I didn't particularly want to go into the army,' he said. 'I didn't fancy walking much.' The difference between ships' officers, like himself, and sea pilots, he said: 'They are birdbrains – they call us anchor-danglers.'

But there was something special about life on the waves. 'If you go to sea in the Merchant Navy or in the Navy, or as a yachtsman, you are in a completely different environment and so you have to function in a different way and relate to people in a different way,' he said. 'The challenge is different and in a sense it's not quite like any other profession – you are segregated in some way. And you are all equally liable to whatever happens. If something happens to your ship everybody on board is equally liable to get hurt.'

Even though he has started his naval career at the age of eighteen, he said: 'I don't think I ever thought of the sea as something to like. It's cold and wet and it's either marvellous or awful. You get lovely weather or there is no winds so you can't sail. The thing is, it's either wonderful because it looks spectacular, you see wonderful sites, but after four years of doing the morning watch I got fed up with watching the sun rise.'

Later he became a trustee of the National Maritime Museum, and said: 'One of the things that is very important is to make sure that the whole of the maritime heritage is displayed in some way.' It was a position he held for over fifty years.

What kept him going is a a a sense of duty – a thing that Prince Philip exemplifies. In 1992, he told the *Independent on Sunday*: 'Everyone has to have a sense of duty. A duty to society, to their family. I mean, you name it. If you haven't got a sense of duty you get the sort of community we have now. Look around: mugging and drugs and abuse, intellectual abuse, intellectual mugging.'

Philip read the biography of Prince Albert as preparation for his role as Prince Consort. It was little help. 'The Prince Consort's position was quite different,' he said. 'Queen Victoria was an executive sovereign, following in a long line of executive sovereigns. The Prince Consort was effectively Victoria's private secretary. But after Victoria the monarchy changed. It became an institution. I had to fit into the institution. I had to avoid getting at cross-purposes, usurping others' authority.'

Otherwise, he was pushed in at the deep end. 'When King George died, there were plenty of people telling me what not to do,' he said. "You mustn't interfere with this." "Keep out." I had to try to support the Queen as best I could, without getting in the way. The difficulty was to find things that might be useful.'

He explained the difficulties to the BBC in 2011 on navigating his role as husband to the soon-to-be-Queen: 'The problem was to recognise what the niche was and to try and grow into it and that was by trial and error... There was no precedent. If I asked somebody, "What do you expect me to do?" they all looked blank. They had no idea, nobody had much idea.'

He found that that was to be his main job – not to get in the way. 'In most cases that was no problem. I did my own thing,' he said. 'Got involved in organisations where I thought I could be useful. The Federation of London Boys' Clubs, the Royal Yachting Association, the MCC. Of course, as long as they were going alright, there wasn't much for me to do. But if an organisation was going bankrupt or had some crisis, then I'd help.'

When asked whether he got much fun out of his royal duties, he said: 'I don't think I think very much about 'fun'. The Variety Club events were fun. The cricket matches for the Playing Fields were fun. The polo was entirely fun.' (The prince was president of the Playing Fields Association for over fifty years after inheriting the position from his uncle Lord Louis Mountbatten. It was granted a royal charter in

1933 by King George V, its first president, and the Queen is patron.)

When he first arrived in Buckingham Palace, he was seen as a 'moderniser'. 'Not for the sake of modernising,' he said, 'not for the sake of buggering about with things. I'm anxious to get things done.'

He shook up the running of Buckingham Palace in the 1950s. 'I introduced a Footman Training Programme... the old boys here hadn't had anything quite like it before. They expected the footmen just to keep on coming. We had an Organisation and Methods Review. I tried to make improvements – without unhinging things.'

He also tackled the age-old custom of the bottle of whisky that appeared by the Queen's bedside every night, even though she had not ordered it. He discovered that Queen Victoria had once had a cold and had asked for a Scotch before bedtime. As the order had never been rescinded, the servants continued to bring whisky every night some eighty years later.

The duke saw himself as a pragmatic facilitator, a banger-together of heads in a manner that can make the most ruthless management consultant seem like a pussyfooter. He dislikes intellectuals, bureaucrats, wafflers, wishy-washy lefties and romantics (yet years later he could open his heart to Princess Diana when she suffered her travail and the hands of the palace machine). And, of course, he hates journalists.

Prince Philip was never much taken in by his

11

opulent surroundings. 'In the first years of the Queen's reign, the level of adulation – you wouldn't believe it,' he said. 'You really wouldn't. It could have been corroding. It would have been very easy to play to the gallery, but I took a conscious decision not to do that. Safer not to be too popular. You can't fall too far.'

He has followed the advice given to him in 1955 by another consort, Prince Bernhard of Netherlands, husband to Queen Juliana: 'Don't let it get you down. In this job, you need a skin like an elephant.'

When Singapore became self-governing in 1959, he told the former colony: 'I have very little personal experience of self-government. I'm one of the most governed people you could hope to meet.' Asked who he most admired, he began by mentioning Bob Menzies, (prime minister of Australia 1939-41 and 1949-66), and Vincent Massey, the (governor-general of Canada 1952-59). Then he stopped: 'No, no, a list would be invidious.'

The prince was only too aware of saying the wrong thing and attempted to make light of it. He told the General Dental Council in 1960: 'Dontopedalogy is the science of opening your mouth and putting your foot in it, a science which I've practised for a good many years.'

In another moment of candid humour, he said: 'I know my reputation is not all that good. If anyone can offer me advice about how I can improve this, or even of any reason why I have this reputation, I shall be more than grateful.'

He was well aware how some of his remarks were received: 'It seems I have a terrible reputation for telling people what they ought to be doing.' And in his book *Men, Machines and Sacred Cows*, he admitted his attempts at humour sometimes fall flat. 'Trying to be funny is a great deal more difficult than trying to be serious,' he said. 'What may strike me as a witty comment can easily turn out to be painfully tactless.'

Considering his image, Philip mused: 'We know there are a number of what are known as image-producing organisations. They produce marvellous images, but no one believes them.'

He was, however, philosophical when he was asked if he was weighed down by the nature of his duties. 'I'm a pragmatist,' he said. 'If I'm here I might as well get on with it. It's no good going around wishing I was doing something else.' Back in the 1960s, he quipped: 'Princely gifts don't come from princes any more. They come from tycoons.' And in an interview with the BBC's Jeremy Paxman he pointed out: 'Any bloody fool can lay a wreath at the thingamy.'

When pressed for his secret for handling so many public appearances, he shot back to the interviewer: 'I never pass up a chance to go to the loo or take a poo.' He also liked to ask the awkward question. 'I suppose I challenge things to stimulate myself and to be stimulating,' he said. 'You don't have to agree with everyone all the time.'

Asked how he would characterise the type of work he did, the prince replied: 'I'm self-employed.' And how did he feel about the people who want to end the monarchy? 'If people feel it has no further part to play, then for goodness sake, let's end the thing on amicable terms without having a row about it.' After all, he famously remarked: 'The art of being a good guest is to know when to leave.'

Always a hard-working member of the royal family, there were moments of relaxations. 'I am interested in leisure in the same way that a poor man is interested in money,' he said. 'I can't get enough of it.'

And when relaxing, Prince Philip admitted self-deprecatingly he was pretty lazy. 'I'm pretty idle really,' he said in the year 2000. 'One reason I took up carriage driving is that I like watching the ponies do all the work.' However he underrates his own contribution to the sport – the development of the bendy pole.

Despite his reputation for never suffering fools gladly, he said that after fifty years he had learnt to suffer fools 'with patience' and even humour it seems.

On his eightieth birthday, the prince was in reflective mood. With a string of divorces and the fire at Windsor Castle the previous decade, the royal family had been going through a tough time. 'I imagine there are a few fortunate souls who have managed to get through life without any anxieties,' he said, 'but my experience is that life has its ups and downs.'

In his ninetieth birthday interview for the BBC, he was asked if he was proud of his achievements. The duke lookeds puzzled. 'No, that's asking too much,' he said. So what of his successes? 'Who cares what I think about it. That's ridiculous.'

When asked whether he was proud of the Duke of Edinburgh Award Scheme, he said: 'I've no reason to be proud. It's satisfying that we've set up a formula that works but I don't run it. It's all fairly second-hand.' He had not even want his name to be attached to it. 'That was against my better judgement,' he said. 'I tried to avoid it but I was overridden.'

In 2001, he had been asked if the Duke of Edinburgh Award scheme would be more popular if it wasn't named after him. 'Whatever you call it, some people will think it is rubbish while some people would not be worried about this connection with this cantankerous old sod up here,' he said.

In his ninetieth birthday interview for ITV, Alan Titchmarsh asked if the prince if he regretted any of his outspokenness. 'Well yes,' the prince said. 'I would rather have not made the mistakes I did make, but I'm not telling you what they were.'

Titchmarsh also had the temerity to ask the prince which of his charities and committees gave him the most joy. 'It's not entertainment,' he said. 'I don't do it for my amusement.'

If he did not already know he was a very important person, Philip discovered it when he was given the freedom of the City of London. The official citation said that the honour was given to 'a person of distinction within the meaning of Section 259 of the Local Government Act, 1933...' The prince remarked: 'It is always comforting to be told that one is a person of distinction. But it is even more comforting to know that it is by Act of Parliament.'

Philip however has no illusions on that front. 'In that splendid language, pidgin English,' he said, 'I'm referred to as fella belong to Mrs Queen.'

Philip on Philip

The Queen's Business

It was Prince Philip's father-in-law George VI who said that the House of Windsor was not a family but a firm. This is a tradition that Philip proudly maintains.

It seems, nonetheless, that he the prince is just as outspoken behind closed doors as he is on the public rostrum. The Queen Mother once asked an official court photographer: 'And how did you find my son-in-law? Difficult, isn't he?'

The Queen

However, he is not a man without sentiment. Recalling meeting his future wife in 1939 when she was thirteen, he said years later: 'You were so shy. I couldn't get a word out of you.'
That shyness hasn't lasted. According to the Queen's former private secretary Lord Charteris: 'It is not unknown for the Queen to tell the Duke to shut up.'

Hours before marrying the princess, Prince Philip asked a friend: 'Am I being very brave or very foolish?'

Reunited with the Queen at the door of Westminster Abbey at the end of the coronation, he observed her crown and asked: 'Where did you get that hat?'

Since the coronation, Prince Philip has spent his life living in the shadow of someone much more revered – The Queen. Rarely does he meet anyone sympathetic to his plight. But once he was visiting a university in Australia where he was introduced to a couple identified as 'Mr & Dr. Robinson.'. The husband explained: 'My wife is a doctor of philosophy and much more important than I am.' Philip replied: 'Ah yes, we have that trouble in our family too.'

The courtiers all say Her Majesty is Queen, but he is in charge behind the wheel. Once he was driving at high speed. The Queen, who was sitting beside him, let her nervousness show by short intakes of breath. 'If you keep on doing that, I will stop the car and put you out,' he said. Later, Lord Mountbatten, who had been sitting in the back seat, asked the Queen why she let herself be spoken to like that. 'You heard what he said,' she replied.

In public, the prince has never shown the Queen up. However, according to *Daily Telegraph* photographer Ian Jones, once – in Belize City – they were going back to the Royal Yacht Britannia and the Queen stopped, chatting on the jetty. 'The Prince stood on the boat and shouted: 'Yak, yak, yak, come on, get a move on.' He suddenly sounded like any other husband teasing the missus,' said Jones.

Although the photographer had followed the royal couple for ten years, at a royal reception at the end of a three-week tour around the Caribbean, the prince enquired: 'Do you live locally?' Correcting his mistake, the Queen said: 'He isn't wearing his cameras tonight.'

The prince's temper is legendary. Once when they were on the Royal Yacht Britannia the Queen was heard to say: 'I'm not coming out of my cabin until he's in a better temper?! I'm going to stay here on my bed until he's better.'

Phillip when allowed out on his own though is entertaining. In Canberra in 1956, he said: 'May I say right away how delighted I am to be back in Australia. The Queen and I have not forgotten the wonderful time we had here three years ago. She had to stay at home this time because I'm afraid she is not quite as free as I am to do as she pleases.'

Stepping into the breach at a Guildhall luncheon given by the Lord Mayor in 1960, he said: 'It is of course a matter of great regret to us all that the

Queen cannot be here today but, as you realise, she has other matters to attend to.' She was giving birth to Prince Andrew. 'When I first heard about your invitation I was naturally flattered and grateful,' he continued. 'For a short while I held the improbable notion that I would get a meal at the Guildhall without making a speech for it, or, at worst, a third of a speech. But I had a feeling this was too good to last and, by what I can only describe as the downright cunning of my relations, I stand before you now.'

Later that year, he was at the opening of a British Exhibition in New York where he explained that he had to curtail his trip to be back in London to attend Trooping the Colour, which occurs each year on the monarch's official birthday. 'Don't ask me to explain why it is that she had an official birthday in June, when her proper birthday is in April. You'll just have to accept it like cricket, pounds, shillings and pence and other quaint, but quite practical, British customs.' If the monarch's consort can't explain it, what hope have the rest of us got?

When asked how you could make the Queen's Christmas message on TV could be made more entertaining, Philip said: 'Short of hiring a line of chorus girls and calling it The Queen Show, what can you do?'

When Prince Philip introduced royal biographer Gyles Brandreth to the Queen, he told her that Brandreth was writing about her. Then the prince leant forward and said: 'Be warned, he's going to cut you to pieces.'

After fifty years of marriage, he said with typical understatement: 'You can take it from me the Queen has the quality of tolerance in abundance.' Ten years later, he said: 'The secret of a happy marriage to have different interests.'

Prince Philip has had lapses about regalia. At the King Baudouin of Belgium's funeral in 1993, he donned the wrong sash. He thought the one he was wearing belonged to the Order of Leopold, the highest order of knighthood in Belgium. It actually belonged to the Order of the Leopard, instituted in 1966 by President Mobutu of the Congo, the colony Belgium reluctantly made independent, and its bitterest enemy.

Princess Margaret

Asked by Scotland Yard to contribute a fingerprint as a souvenir of a visit, he replied: 'Let's choose an interesting finger.' Then he was told that they already had Princess Margaret's fingerprints. 'Good for you,' he said.

22

Prince Philip on Prince Philip

Prince Charles

On being a father, he said: 'As a parent, you can either try to compete with your children or you can feel proud of them. I've opted for the latter.' And he was sympathetic to their plight. Concerning his children's careers, he said: 'I don't think people appreciate that there aren't a great many options open to them. I suppose they could go into the church. But what experience seems to show is that if they enter any commercial or competitive activity, the people inevitably pick on them as the source of unfair competition.'

On a Canadian tour, he was asked whether he knew the Scilly Isles. 'Yes,' he said. 'My son owns them.' Freehold of the islands are owned by the Duchy of Cornwall. Rent on the houses the Duchy owns there brings Prince Charles a substantial income.

Of the Prince of Wales, he said: 'He's a romantic, and I'm a pragmatist. That means we do see things differently.' After a reflective pause, he continued: 'And because I don't see things as a romantic would, I'm unfeeling.'

Perhaps father and son were not as close as they could be. The Queen and Prince Philip were once scheduled to have lunch with Prince Charles on board the Royal Yacht *Britannia* which was moored in the Thames to celebrate their beloved son's birthday. On the way, they made a visit to a hostel for the homeless run by the charity Centre Point. Signing the visitors' book there, Philip asked: 'What's the date today? Is it the thirteenth?' The Queen replied testily: 'No, it's the fourteenth… Charles's birthday, remember?' Presumably, Charles's present was a rain check.

Princess Anne

Maybe Prince Philip was closer to his daughter. In 1970, he said of the twenty-year-old Princess Anne: 'If it doesn't fart or eat hay, she isn't interested.'

Duke of Windsor

Prince Philip was worried that, by marrying commoners, the royal family might become 'too ordinary.' However, he was happy that they mixed with people of all social classes. After all, Britain is not as hidebound as it once was. 'People think there's a rigid class system here,' he said in 2000, 'but dukes have even been known to marry chorus girls. Some have even married Americans.' This was worthy of P.G. Wodehouse, but was widely interpreted as a swipe at Edward VIII and Wallis Simpson, later the Duke and Duchess of Windsor.

Prince Andrew

24

On the announcement of Prince Andrew's engagement to Sarah Ferguson in 1986, the Duke of Edinburgh said: 'I'm delighted he's getting married, but not because I think it will keep him out of trouble because, in fact, he's never been in trouble in the sense the popular press would have it.' (There was that business with soft-porn star Koo Stark.)

After the couple split up, Prince Philip said of Sarah Ferguson: 'Her behaviour was a bit odd.' Then after a sigh, he said: 'But I'm not vindictive. I am not vindictive... I don't see her because I don't see much point.'

The prince had foreseen the break-up back in 1986. Just before they were married, he told Andrew: 'I think she'll be a great asset. For one thing, she is capable of becoming self-employed.' And perhaps, for a moment, Philip thought it had all come horribly true. In 2001, at a reception at the Guards' Polo Club – of which he is president – his flow of wit was interrupted by a flame-haired waitress proffering cocktail sausages. 'Good God, I can't take canápes from you – you're Fergie!' roared Philip. As the poor girl slunk away, her red face matching her hair, the prince turned back to his party guests, guffawing, and said: 'She's working anywhere for money now!'

To mark death of the Queen Mother, it was suggested that Prince Philip be elevated to become a knight of the Royal Victoria Order. Philip rejected the offer saying it was 'an order for servants.' Despite this, in 2003, Prince Andrew was made a Knight Commander of the Royal Victorian Order. Then, in a private ceremony at Buckingham Palace in 2011, the Queen invested Andrew as a Knight of the Grand Cross of the Royal Victorian Order, the highest rank of the order, to add to his glittering array of honours and medals before the two of them settled down for tea.

Prince Edward

When Prince Edward was accepted into Jesus College Cambridge, despite only obtaining a C and two Ds at A-level, his father quipped: 'What a friend we have in Jesus.'

When comedian Aaron Barschak gate-crashed Prince William's twenty-first birthday party at Windsor Castle wearing a pink dress, false beard and a turban like that worn by Osama bin Laden, Prince Edward was the only one of the senior royals not present. So if Barschak had been a suicide bomber, Edward would have succeeded to the throne. After Barschak had stormed the stage and got himself arrested, Philip told guests that Edward must have been behind the stunt. 'It's bound to have been

Edward,' he said. 'Only the boy could have coached such a rotten performance out of someone.'

The Extended Family

As the ranks of the royal family swelled, Prince Philip was the prime mover behind the Palace's Way Ahead Group, the regular meetings of senior members of the royal family. 'We have to co-ordinate,' he said. 'Don't forget, at the beginning of the Queen's reign there were just one or two of us doing things, but then the children grew up and instead of one or two we had ten or twelve. People were tripping over one another. We got them to specialise in their interests. Charles went off to the arts, Anne went off to prisons. It's about an efficient use of resources.'

Prince Philip is even defensive about the ancient members of the firm. When royal biographer Lady Antonia Fraser was invited to lunch at Buckingham Palace, the Duke of Edinburgh asked her what she was writing. She replied: 'The Six Wives of Henry VIII.' He grew angry and said: 'Why do people always say Henry VIII and his six wives as though it was all one word? There is plenty more to say about Henry.' She replied cravenly: 'Oh yes, sir, there is, I mean he was a wonderful musician.' At this, the duke grew even crosser: 'He was a wonderful military strategist, a fighter, he bashed the French.'

For emphasis, he repeated: 'He bashed the French.' (Sadly, this is not entirely true. According to the Encyclopaedia Britannica: 'Henry himself displayed no military talent.' His victory against the Scots at Flodden was won by the Earl of Surrey. His campaigns in France were organised by Cardinal Wolsey and resulted in 'the greatness of England in Europe… being shown up as a sham'.)

In 2012, Prince Philip spoke of his fears for the future of the firm. At a luncheon for American journalists, he said: 'The more accessible you become, the more ordinary you become. The argument could be that if you are ordinary, what are you doing anyway?'

There are, as yet, no fears that Prince Philip will ever become ordinary.

Education

Prince Philip and education are not natural bedfellows by any stretch of the imagination. Talking about his school days, he said in 1965: 'My favourite subject at school was avoiding unnecessary work.' This certainly did not hold him back in his chosen career.

Honorary Titles

Although he never attended university, the prince is burdened down by a growing number honorary degrees and titles. Accepting an honorary doctorate in science from Reading University, he told the faculty on the subject: 'It must be pretty well known that I never earned an honest degree in my life and I certainly never made any effort to gain an honorary one.' So, understandably, he told an audience at the University of Salford: 'The best thing to do with a degree is to forget it.'

When he was installed as chancellor of the University of Edinburgh, where he had previously been awarded an honorary doctorate in law, he concluded his address by saying: 'You may think that I have spent rather a long time laying down the law with very little justification. May I remind you then that the last time I was in this hall I was given full permission to teach law in any university in Christendom, so you only have yourselves to blame.' He took the opportunity to give Dr Kurt Hahn, his old headmaster at Gordonstoun an honorary doctorate in laws. 'It cannot be given to many to have the opportunity and desire to heap honours upon their former headmaster.'

Addressing American students, he said that he was rather jealous of those who got a Fulbright scholarship and spent a year in America, and added 'I don't suppose chancellors of universities qualify, or, perhaps, honorary doctors of law.'

Addressing the Royal College of Art in July 1955, the prince said: 'I think perhaps the college should warn future honorary fellows of the ordeal they will have to undergo in being made to wear flannel dressing gowns.'

Prince Philip has so many honorary appointments that it is not surprising that he gets a little mixed up. In February 2003, he told guests at the University of York: 'It is surprising the way things have changed since I first became chancellor fifty years ago.' The university was celebrating its fortieth anniversary at that time and its chancellor was opera singer Dame Janet Baker. Philip was then chancellor of Cambridge University where he had served for thirty-three years.

University

Addressing an audience at the opening of a £500,000 extension to what was then Heriot-Watt College in Edinburgh in 1957, Prince Philip jumped into the debate that was going on about education with both feet. 'There is, quite rightly, a very lively argument about general education in schools and universities,' he said. 'The parties to the argument are legion – there are the vocationalists, the humanists, the specialists and the generalists and then, of course, there are a lot of people like me with little knowledge but a ready opinion on occasions such as this.'

Later that day the prince got into a lift that got stuck between two floors. 'This could only happen in a technical college,' he said.

On a visit during the Golden Jubilee visit to the University of East London he asked a Polish student whether once he had finished his course he would be going back to Poland to corrupt the Polish people. Then, when told that a member of staff was not a lecturer said: 'That's right, you do not have enough hair to be a lecturer.'

While many were ruing the current 'brain drain' of British scientists to America, the prince said it was 'a very nice compliment to our educational system.'

In May 2013 at the opening of the £212-million Medical Research Council's Laboratory of Molecular Biology in Cambridge, the Prince Philip asked a Polish scientist: 'Did you come here to pick raspberries?'

Opening the £556-million maths centre at Cambridge University in July 2000, he told an amused audience: 'This is a lot less expensive than the Dome, and I think it's going to be a lot more useful.' (Renamed The O2 and given a £600-million facelift, the London Millenium Dome is now a surprisingly popular sports and entertainment venue.)

Schools

Being a parent, he has a firm idea of what schools are for. At the official opening of the Joy and Stanley Cohen Hertsmere Jewish Primary School in Hertfordshire in 2000, the children had been recalled from the summer holidays to sing to him. 'Holidays are curious things, aren't they?' said the prince. 'You send children to school to get them out of your hair. Then they come back and make life difficult for parents. That is why holidays are set so they are just about the limit of your endurance. Then you send them back to school again.'

He expressed similar feelings when in 2013 he met Malala Yousafzai, the heroic fifteen-year-old schoolgirl shot in the head by Taliban extremists in Pakistan for encouraging girls to go to school. 'There's a thing about children going to school,' he said. 'They go to school because the parents don't want them in the house.' She laughed at his joke and explained she had missed a day of school to attend the reception at Buckingham Palace. 'I had to miss school because I was meeting the Queen,' she said. 'It's such an honour for me to be here at Buckingham Palace. It's really an honour to meet the Queen.'

Visiting Queen Anne's school in Reading, Berkshire, he said of the girls' blood-red uniforms: 'It makes you all look like Dracula's daughters!'

Visiting Linacre Primary School in Bootle, Merseyside, in 1998, he asked a caretaker: 'Can you manage to control all these vandals?' Chief boom-wielder Jim Kampsell defended the pupils, saying: 'We don't have any vandals, they all come from outside.' The duke was particularly touchy about vandals after the Prince of Wales accused him of vandalism for felling a three-mile stretch of oaks, limes and chestnut in Windsor Great Park. 'They're an eyesore,' said Prince Philip. Among his many roles, he is Ranger of Windsor Great Park. 'I'm a sort of godfather of the whole business,' he said.

Advice on What to Do

Addressing the children at a school in Ipswich, he told the pupils: 'It is traditional on these occasions for me to give you a bit of advice, which you will equally traditionally ignore.' Recalling his own school days, he said he remembered 'thinking what a lot of nonsense visiting persons managed to talk. Of course, I know now that all their addresses were really quite brilliant. I've more or less got to say that or I shall be accused of letting down the Union.'

After fifty years of involvement with universities, in 1997, he told penniless twenty-one-year-old Alison Nisbet, a student at Edinburgh University: 'Why don't you go and live in a hostel to save cash?'

In 2001, thirteen-year-old Andrew Adams was a summer school at Salford University where the NOVA British space project is based. He was admiring one of the rockets when the Duke of Edinburgh asked him if he would like to travel into space. When he said yes, the Duke told him: 'You'll have to lose a little bit of weight first. You're too fat to be an astronaut.' The forthright help on what to do was taken lightly – the teenager said he wanted to become an actor.

On formal education in general, he remarks: 'University is merely so much vocational training unless it puts some fire in your belly.'

Openings

Early in his career of cutting ribbons, he discovered that the official opening often occurred sometime after the establishment was already up and running. Opening a school in Buckinghamshire in 1958, he said: 'I always find these openings rather strange occasions and I gather I'm something like nine months late. I don't think you need worry. I think that the fact that school has been operating without being properly opened won't necessarily have any ill effect on you.'

He developed this thought further when opening the Chesterfield College of Technology. 'A lot of time and energy has been spent on arranging for you to listen to me take a long time to declare open a building, which everybody knows is open already,' he said. 'Tomorrow, to all intents and purposes, everything will be back to normal. That rather makes it look as if we are all wasting our time...'

In the 1960s Philip argued: 'I try to avoid laying inaugural stones because of their habit of getting lost, abandoned or stolen.' Laying the foundation stone of Delhi Engineering College 1959, he said: 'I have to admit that I was in two minds about accepting this kind invitation. You see there is a sort of myth that members of the royal family do nothing else but open things and lay foundation stones, and I don't want to add any substance to that idea.' Then he apologised for only laying one stone: 'It won't make any difference anyway because the value of the college will lay in its graduates and not in it stones.' On another occasion, he apologised for laying a foundation stone crooked, but said the builders would lay the rest straighter.

Asked about universities back in 1983, he said: 'The first five hundred years of any institution are always the most difficult.'

In 1958, presenting a Charter of Incorporation to St Edmund Hall, Oxford, Philip said: 'In five hundred years from now, you will be able to put the charter on display and say that it was presented five hundred years ago. That, in my experience, is what usually happens and it is always most impressive because by that time the seal is usually missing and the writing is both illegible and unintelligible anyway.' He strongly advised them to look after the charter 'because, throughout history, a document of some sort had always been looked upon as a sort of passport to respectability and, without it, you will never be able to prove – whatever it is you want to prove.'

In 1957, he told Manchester College of Science and Technology: 'I wish this college every possible success and, to show that these are not empty words, I have agreed to become Visitor to the College. In my case, this is the only title I possess which means exactly what it says.'

On the opening of the David Keir Building at Queen's University in Belfast in 1959, he said: 'I know that it is more usual to complain about governments than to praise them, but in this case the least we can do is to acknowledge that the Northern Ireland Government has contributed no less than £2 million towards this project – even if it is the taxpayers' money.'

Unveiling a plaque at the University of Hertfordshire's new Hatfield campus in November 2003, he said: 'During the Blitz a lot of shops had their windows blown in and sometimes they put up notices saying, 'More open than usual.' I now declare this place more open than usual.' It is a quip he had used on several occasions.

In 2005, when Bristol University's engineering facility had been closed down so that he could open it, he rued: 'It doesn't look like much work goes on at this University.'

Plymouth University's new marine building in 2012,

he said: 'It's now quite a long time since I started my university career. But unlike most people, I started at the wrong end. I became chancellor of the University of Wales in 1947 and been going downhill ever since.'

Privilege

Given the gulf between state education and the public schools, there is a certain amount of privilege involved in education. But Prince Philip is equivocal on the subject: 'Up to quite recently, it was thought one gets into a university by paying, but now there is another privilege – intellectual privilege, which is another mistake. Privilege is privilege whether it is due money or intellect or whether you have six toes.'

He certainly did not feel privileged when he was at school. 'I was not the least aware I was any different from any of the others. It's true I had this title of Prince, but it's surprising how you can live it down.'

Prince Philip was not university-educated and he famously declared that he did not feel in the least diminished by missing out on higher education: 'I am one of those stupid bums that never went to university,' he told a group of students in the 1980s, 'and a fat lot of harm it did me.'

On such occasions as award ceremonies, royalty are the recipients of a certain amount of flattery. Prince

Philip was aware of this and, when accepting an honorary doctorate in 1960, said: 'Some people might well feel that your vice-chancellor has succeeded in presenting me for this honorary degree, not just in a good light, but in a positively rosy glow of perfection. I can only imagine that he has taken Disraeli's advice that "Everyone like flattery; and when you come to royalty you should lay it on with a trowel."'

Viewing toilets

Visiting the University of East London during the Golden Jubilee, Prince Philip was shown an environmentally friendly toilet which is flushed with air instead of water. He asked: 'Where does the wind come from?' He then raised a laugh when he was shown pellets of sewage and fluid ash as part of a demonstration of sewage recycling. 'What do they eat in East London to get that?' he asked.

When shown lavatory cisterns in the London Design Centre, he put his environmental hat on said: 'This is the biggest waste of water in the country by far. You spend half-a-pint and flush two gallons.'

Sports

In his sporting life, the Prince has played soccer as goalie, field hockey as centre forward, squash, badminton and rugby. He was captain of the Gordonstoun Cricket XI. 'But there were only about twenty of us at the school,' he said.

No Laughing Matter

Bemoaning the decline of school sports, the prince said: 'Taking part in games and sports is very much part of the growing-up process. Taking part particularly in team games – or any games that have rules and regulations and involve more than just a contest between two people – teaches a respect for the law because you won't have a game unless you play according to the rules, and that is quite a good thing to learn.'

The prince is a great believer in the old-fashioned virtues of physical education. 'The great difficulty that schools have is that the old PE teacher, the gym mistresses and sports masters and things, have tended to hardly exist anymore,' he said. 'They have closed down all the special PE schools. I think that has been a sad loss.' It is not hard to believe that the prince was a particular fan of the gym mistress.

On the value of losing, the prince wisely remarks: 'I think it [sport] also teaches that failure isn't the end of the world. You always bounce back again, and you may win next time. The idea that you are somehow depressed and you go and shoot yourself if you lose is ridiculous. It is very important through life that you don't win all the time: occasionally you have to face a defeat.'

According to Prince Philip, the competitive urge is a natural inclination: 'Everything you do is based on competition unless some half-witted teacher seems to think it's bad for you,' he said. 'People like to pit their abilities against someone else. People want to race each other. It's what gives the whole thing spice.'

Idle Hands

Generally, the prince is impatient with inactivity. He was chatting with the Duke of Beaufort one night at Badminton, when he said: 'It seems a great pity in all these horse shows that they only have jumping and show classes for children. They just sit there, all dressed up. They don't get much fun out of it. Can't we think of something the ordinary pony can do? The family pony. It may look like nothing on earth, but it's a great favourite.' This was the origin of the Pony Club Mounted Games, which was modelled on the Army's gymkhana.

The prince is not much one for sitting on the sidelines. 'I am not really a talented spectator, frankly,' he says. 'Yes, it's quite fun to watch but it's not the be-all and end-all. I've had enough of it.'

Balls to You

After a banquet in Brazil, the president of the national bowling club made a short speech in Portuguese. Realising that Prince Philip did not understand it, he made an effort to summon up his entire English vocabulary when presenting the emblem of the club to the prince and said: 'Balls, you know.' The Prince graciously replied: 'And balls to you, sir.'

Sometimes such childlike humour cannot be avoided, like when Prince Philip was lecturing the president of the World Bank, Tom Clausen, on the necessary of adding an environmental clause to the bank's loan agreements. Under his breath, Clausen muttered: 'Balls.' 'What did you say?' asked the Prince. 'I said it is difficult,' said Clausen, amending his comment. 'No you didn't,' corrected Philip. 'You said 'balls.' And what's more, sir, I say balls to you.' They dissolved in giggling.

Prince Philip's forthright manner encourages plain speaking in others. Visiting the British team at the Mexico Olympics in 1968, the prince was quick to assure everyone that the lack of oxygen at that altitude was nothing to worry about – he had played some gruelling polo matches there in the past and quickly became acclimatised. The boxer Chris Finnegan put his hand up and said: 'You know when you said you never felt any problem with the lack of oxygen during your tough polo matches? Well I was thinking – did anyone think of asking the bleedin' horses?'

At a reception at Buckingham Palace for the British athletes who had won forty-two gold medals at the 2008 Beijing Paralympics, he told twenty-four-year-old medal winner Matt Shelham that there was gold in the room and that some of it should be donated to Gordon Brown to help with the country's financial crisis.

Sailing

The Prince's greatest love was, of course, sailing. Heaping praise on his yachting companion and boat designer Uffa Fox, Prince Philip said: 'I am as surprised to see him made a Royal Designer for Industry as no doubt he is to see me president of the Royal Society of Arts. There is a tendency nowadays to imagine that everything new must be scientific or rational… I can state categorically that there is practically nothing scientific or rational about Mr Fox.'

Cricket

Later in life, at a charity match, he had England player Tom Graveney caught at fine leg from an off-break. 'He was doing very well when I was put on to bowl,' said the Prince. 'I was trying to bowl off-breaks and I thought well, with any luck he might snick something on the leg side, which he did. Unfortunately, for him, someone was standing there and caught it.' The Prince added: 'He, of course, was then unmercifully teased by all his contemporaries. Every time I met him afterwards I always tactfully failed to mention it and he always brought it up.' It was, he conceded, 'just one wicket.'

Philip told a cricket club conference: 'The last time I played in a village match I was given out l.b.w. first ball. That is the sort of umpiring that should be looked into.'

When Brian Johnston asked Prince Philip on *Test Match Special* if there was anything he would like to change about modern cricket, the prince replied: 'I only wish that sometimes their trousers fitted better.'

In 1999, at a Buckingham Palace reception for one-day cricket World Cup, a white Zimbabwean player lined up with the West Indians. 'Aren't you in the wrong team?' asked the prince. 'No,' said the interloper. 'I play for Zimbabwe but I'm hung like a West Indian.' There was much merriment all round.

Prince Philip is patron and honorary twelfth man of the Lord's Taverners, a cricketing charity found in 1950 by a group of actors who enjoyed a pint while watching cricket from the Tavern pub at Lord's Cricket Ground. In 1962, he wrote the preface to Leslie Frewin's miscellany *The Boundary Book* which raised over £5,000 for the National Play Fields Association, which the prince has been president of for over fifty years after inheriting the post from his uncle Lord Mountbatten. In the preface, he said: 'I cannot claim to have an intimate knowledge of the Lord's Tavern but I do know that it has an atmosphere that cannot be ascribed to cricket alone! Quite what it has that make the Tavern such a very special place, I don't know. But there is something about this celebrated hostelry that can persuade an eminent Scottish playwright to stand and watch cricket in the company of perfectly strange Englishmen. What is it that causes staid theatrical producers to finish rehearsals early on some trivial excuse, only to find themselves, ten minutes later, rubbing shoulders at the Tavern with their own actors who should be studying their lines? And what prompts a renowned conductor to lay down his baton on a Saturday afternoon and look for a cab to St John's Wood?

Just cricket? Scientists one day may discover what controls the homing instinct of fish and birds but I hope they never try to analyse the urge of the Taverner to return to Lord's.'

In *The Boundary Book: Second Innings* published in 1986, His Royal Twelfthmanship went on to explain: 'Those readers who are unfamiliar with the Lord's Taverners should know that it is a heterogeneous collection of cricket enthusiasts who prefer to watch their favourite game from a public house with a view of Lord's cricket ground rather than from a seat in the stands. As might be expected, the members of the Lord's Taverners are, to put it mildly, different. For some hitherto unexplained reason, it seems that the members of those professions engaged in entertaining the public appear to requite the comfort of a full tankard in order to enjoy a game of cricket.' The pub has since been demolished to make way for the new Tavern Stand, though a new Tavern pub was opened on the ground in 1967.

Introduced to the Australian test team at Lord's in 2009, Prince Philip asked Aussie head coach Tim Nielsen if he was the team's scorer. This was said to have caused 'much amusement to the rest of the touring party.'

An MCC official asked the prince if he had enjoyed his lunch. Philip said: 'Why do you ask that?' MCC man said: 'I hoped the answer would be yes.' To which Philip replied: 'What a stupid question.'

Polo

In 1965, Philip remarked: 'The only active sport I follow is polo – and most of the work is done by the pony.' However, he described polo umpires as 'mutton-headed dolts totally ignorant of the simplest rules of the game.' But then, perhaps he was biased.

When times get hard, even the royal family feels the pinch. In 1969, the Duke of Edinburgh rued on American TV: 'We go into the red next year, I shall probably have to give up polo.' As it was, after twenty years in the saddle, he retired from playing polo in 1971.

Polo is no laughing matter. On a visit to Pakistan, he turned down an offer to play, explaining later: 'I went to Pakistan on serious business. If I'd gone there to play polo, I'd have got in some practice beforehand.'

Carriage Driving

When Prince Philip took up carriage driving, he was head of the International Equestrian Federation.

'One of the executive members from Poland said to me, 'Do you know we ought to have rules for carriage driving? Because it's becoming very popular,' he explained. 'I'd never heard of carriage driving so I decided to have a look. I went to Germany. It was electrifying to see something like twenty-four carriages going round the ring. Then I thought, well, we've got some horses, we've got some carriages, why don't I have a go? In 1973 I entered my first national competition, and to my horror I was told I could compete in the European Championships in May that year as an individual. I did and I was rather impressed. Things went quite well until I hit the last obstacle, which damaged the carriage to such an extent I had to retire before the end. However, I had a clear round in the cones, so I was not last, at least.'

Prince Philip said that he then took up carriage-driving because it was a 'geriatric sport.' 'I thought of it as a retirement exercise. I promise you, when I set out I thought it would be a nice weekend activity, rather like a golfing weekend. Which it was, until some idiot asked me to be a member of the British team.'

In 2011, he gave a fuller explanation of his interest in carriage-driving. 'I gave up polo when I was fifty,' he said, 'and then this started and I thought, 'Well, you've got horses and carriages, why don't you have a go?' So I started in 1973 and it's been going on since then. These were carriage horses from London – they'd never been through anything bigger than a puddle. I made a little crossing – a stream, and had to bribe them across. I sent my groom across the other side with a jar of sugar – and they decided to get their feet wet!'

When competing in a carriage race with other teams in 1974, his carriage hit a tree and overturned. He was then asked if he enjoyed carriage driving. 'Don't be a fool,' he replied. 'Do you think I do it for penance?' He was asked whether he would like to compete in another event: 'Do you have another team of horses?', came the innocent enquiry. 'Another team?' the prince retorted. 'Do you think they grow on trees?'

At a meeting of the International Equestrian Federation in Geneva, a Chinese delegate asked Prince Philip about protocol. He was not fussy: 'As far as we are concerned, you can play Colonel Bogey and fly a pair of knickers from the flagpole as your team enters the arena,' he said.

The prince has won two team gold medals at World Championships (in 1974 and 1980). He admits his proudest moment was winning the four-in-hand individual title at Windsor, with a team of bays, in 1982, although he said: 'It was very satisfying, but the only reason I won was because George Bowman

Senior [multiple world champion, team and individual] came a cropper somewhere.'

These were the days when the Prince competed with horses, but there came a time when he felt he should reduce the horsepower a little. 'In 1986, I came to the conclusion I was the oldest person on the horse teams circuit, having done five World Championships and God knows how many Europeans,' he said. 'I'd already been driving ponies at Balmoral, so I decided to go on with them.'

Horses sometimes get the rough side of the Duke's tongue. At the carriage-driving competition in the Lowther Horse Driving Trials, Prince Philip grew red-faced as he struggled to keep control of his horses. 'Come on, you bloody idiots,' he exclaimed within earshot of shocked spectators. 'It was marvellous,' said one. 'He was just like his Spitting Image character.'

Walking across a muddy field at the Lowther trials in 2008, he said: 'It was like walking on a fat lady's tummy.' The event had to be cancelled that year, due to heavy rain.

Philip's enthusiasm for carriage driving sometimes wanes: 'You've got to be a nutcase to do this. The best bit is when it's all over,' he complains. After a particularly frustrating day at the reins in 2006, he said: 'I want to shoot the lot of them. Then myself.'

When asked how he liked to relax, sport was not the first thing to come to mind: 'Relax? Have dinner and go to bed,' he said. At eighty-five, it's no surprise he considered retiring from carriage driving: 'You'd be surprised how much work it is. You've got to practise like mad and it's absolutely bloody exhausting.'

Asked if his driving got in the way of his duties, he said: 'It's the other way round. The duties get in the way of the driving.'

Elf and Safety

One interviewer pointed out that Philip's favourite sport was not the gentle kind that most elderly people took up, like crown green bowls or pub darts. 'It is a bit risky, isn't it, for the consort of the Queen in his mid-eighties?' she asked. Spluttered the prince, impatiently: 'Saying, "Oh it's a very dangerous sport." You haven't got a bloody clue, have you?' She admitted she had not. 'You've never seen anybody come to any harm, so why do you say it's dangerous? It's like climbing. People say, 'Oh, you can fall off.' Well, they don't fall off. Not if they learn properly and if they're properly organised. It's not dangerous. It's dangerous for people who don't know the first thing about it. If I were to put you on the carriage, of course you would get into trouble. And if you were to climb Everest, again you'd get into trouble. So you've got to see risk in relation to ability. When did anybody take their eye out playing conkers?'

Prince Philip is a vocal opponent to health and safety harridans and has suffered remarkably few mishaps in a carriage career that has spanned three decades. Of his rare accidents, he plainly says: 'I turned over years ago when I hit a stump,' he said. 'And once, in practice, a pole on the carriage broke, so you're pretty helpless then. I was thrown and kicked on the way out.'

When it came to fitness, the prince bluntly acknowledges: 'I've been lucky. I've had very few things go wrong. It's terrible for people who break things. Take [Wayne] Rooney' (who had just fractured a metatarsal) – 'that must be really hideous for him at the high point of his career.' What did he think of Theo Walcott as Wayne Rooney's replacement in the England squad? 'No idea. I don't have opinions about things I know nothing about.'

Football

Generally, Philip has little respect for football. During an interview for the *Daily Telegraph*, he asked journalist Sue Mott what she did for fun. When she replied with 'watching football,' he inquired: 'Don't you actually do anything? Shove-ha'penny or something?'

During a visit to Uruguay in 1962, the Prince declared: 'I am convinced that the greatest contribution Britain has made to the national life of Uruguay was teaching the people football.'

Although watching football is not something he finds entertaining, it sometimes inspires his own recreations. Once when eyeing Nottingham Forest Football Club's trophies, he
pondered: 'I suppose I'd get in trouble if I were to melt them down.'

It seems he was out of his depth when it came to the beautiful game. In 1964, when Chelsea captain Terry Venables introduced him to a new player who would be 'playing his first game,' Philip
replied: 'You mean he has never played football before?'

At Arsenal's Highbury stadium, Prince Philip was introduced to Leeroy Thornhill, a musician from the group The Prodigy, who was part of the club's celebrity team. He was wearing a replica shirt with the name of the sponsor Sega Dreamcast on it. Philip asked: 'Is Dreamcast the name of the team?'

Visiting the Krishna-Avanti Primary School, Mo Kassamali, the coach of a local football team, asked the ninety-year-old prince if he wanted to come for a quick training session. The prince declined with the excuse: 'The old heart's not working.'

No go areas

Before the Olympic Games in 1948, he told an audience: 'I wish to contradict a rumour. You will not see a familiar figure bearing the Olympic torch on the opening day.'

Asked whether he fancied bungee jumping, the Prince sassed: 'No, I don't think I'd like my eyeballs to go out and then in again, somehow.'

At a golfing society dinner in 1949, he prefaced his address with the statement: 'Prepare for a shock – I do not play golf.'

The Spur of the Moment

Prince Philip reserves much of his wit to leaven what would otherwise be the dreary round of official openings, garden parties, awards ceremonies and receptions. Needless to say, even when performing his official duties there is never a dull moment. Royal rota Cameraman Peter Wilkinson has a tried-and-true game plan: 'Whenever I lose him in a crowd, I just listen out for the laughter and then I find him. He loves making people laugh.'

Robes

On the steps of St. Paul's Cathedral during the Silver Jubilee celebrations, a sudden gust of wind caught the ermine-trimmed robes of the Lord Mayor of London, Sir Robin Gillett, blowing them up like a balloon. 'Look, I think the Lord Mayor is taking off,' Prince Philip said to the Queen.

In 1965, Prince Philip caused a minor controversy when he described the ceremonial robes of the councillors in Ryde as 'dressing gowns.' Not to be confused with his own dressing gowns, with his royal crest embroidered on the chest.

Eating

When the newly appointed Mayor of Slough David Macisaac first met Prince Philip at a Duke of Edinburgh Awards ceremony, the prince asked him if he was going to put on weight 'with all the meals you attend as mayor.' Macisaac said he hoped not. Prince Philip patted him on his stomach simply saying, 'We will see.' At the opening of East Berkshire College in Maidenhead a few months later, the prince patted him on the stomach again, which was now much larger: 'I told you you would get fat!'

Beards

In his younger days, Prince Philip sported a remarkably bushy beard – an achievement it seems no one can match. At a garden party at Buckingham Palace in 2009, the prince spotted Stephen Judge, who was sporting a small sculpted beard. 'What do you do?' asked Philip. 'I'm a designer, sir,' Judge replied. 'Well, you're obviously not a hirsute designer,' the prince added. Seeing that the man was crushed, Philip tried to revive the conversation by saying: 'Well, you didn't design your beard too well, did you? If you are going to grow a beard, grown a beard. You really must try harder.'

The beard of composer Simon Bainbridge was another to come under criticism by the prince. At a reception at the Royal Academy, the prince remarked on the sparseness of Bainbridge's beard compared to the luxuriant growth of his hair: 'Why don't you go the whole hog?' he asked.

Abilities

On a visit to Bromley in 2012, the Duke spotted eighty-nine-year-old wheelchair-bound Barbara Dubery who was wrapped in a foil blanket to keep warm. 'Are they going to put you in the oven next?' he asked.

Not one to worry about offending, his potential for wheelchair jokes seems endless. The prince once asked wheelchair-bound Jackie Henderson: 'Do people trip over you?' And of her electric wheelchair he said: 'Do you need a licence for that?' At a Buckingham Palace garden party, he asked a paraplegic: 'Why do you have a stick if you're in a wheelchair?' At another garden party, wheelchair-bound James Banfield was told: 'That's the best way to get around this place.' Twenty-nine-year-old Sandie Hollands, who suffers from a muscle-wasting disease, was told: 'You are a bit of a menace in that thing.' She was shocked and replied: 'I can assure you I am a good driver and not a menace.' He pointed to the metal footrests and said: 'They catch people's ankles.' When she told him that she did not hit people's ankles, he smiled.

Visiting Redbridge House in London on the Diamond Jubilee tour, Prince Philip was introduced to sixty-year-old David Miller who had a spinal problem that made walking difficult. Pointing to his four-wheeled mobility scooter, the Prince said: 'How many people have you knocked over this morning on that thing?' – prompting laughter from both Mr. Miller and the crowd. Philip cracked the same gag later when he met the mayor of Waltham Forest, Geoff Walker, who has cerebral palsy and also uses a mobility scooter. But the councillor saw the funny side. 'I told him 'no, I had not knocked anyone down," he said.

Always one to offer advice, in 2013 Prince Philip jokingly told a double amputee that he should put wheels on his prosthetic limbs to move around quicker. On another occasion, Prince Philip inquired of a soldier who had been wounded by a ball-bearing bomb: 'When you shake your head, it doesn't rattle?'

Prince Philip is just as keen to exchange a quip with the blind. During the Golden Jubilee tour in 2002, he spotted fifty-five-year-old Susan Edwards waiting outside Exeter Cathedral with her guide dog Natalie, and said: 'I understand they now have eating dogs for the anorexic.' Ms Edwards had been virtually blind for seventeen years and did not take offence.

In 2002, Stephen Menary, a teenage army cadet nearly blinded in a Real IRA bomb, was introduced to the Queen and Prince Philip at a tree-planting event in Hyde Park as part of the Golden Jubilee celebrations. When the Queen asked the fifteen-year-old how much sight he had, the prince promptly responded: 'Not a lot, judging by the tie he's wearing.' A year after the incident, Stephen was on parade at the Jubilee celebrations going past Buckingham Palace and flashed a giant Union Jack tie as if to say: 'This one is even worse!'

In March 2003, fourteen-year-old George Barlow wrote to the Queen inviting her to Romford, Essex. Prince Philip accompanied the Queen on her visit. When introduced to the teenager, he said: 'Ah, you're the one who wrote the letter. So you can write then? Ha, ha. Well done.' Afterwards, George said that meeting the Queen was a great honour, while Buckingham Palace said the duke 'would never have inferred in any way the boy was stupid'.

At a Police Rehabilitation and Retraining Trust in County Down in 2009, Prince Philip was introduced to a shirtless seventy-nine-year-old former RUC man who was receiving physiotherapy treatment for injuries he had sustained in the Troubles. 'All that pushing and pulling, bloody agony,' said the prince, waving his arms. 'It is hard to say whether physios actually do anything.' He added: 'I hope you don't get pneumonia in the process.' And as for acupuncture: 'If someone tried that with me, they'd have no luck.'

The Public

Visiting a comprehensive in Sheffield that used to have one of the worst academic records, the duke said to two of the mums: 'Were you here in the bad old days? That's why you can't read and write then!'

An honorary Air Commodore, Prince Philip was in full RAF uniform when he visited RAF Kinloss where three squadrons were being disbanded due to defence cuts in 2011. When one of the air staff who was leaving the service told him that she was going to be a dental nurse, he shot back: 'It'll be like pulling teeth.' The other told him that she was going to work on the future development of the base. 'You're going to have to have a very good imagination then,' he quipped.

In 1975, the traditional Maundy Money (special silver coins given to selected pensioners on the Thursday before Easter) was distributed at Peterborough Cathedral. Until 1965, when the city of Peterborough was merged with the county of Huntingdon, the Soke of Peterborough was a county in its own right – *soke* being the Old English word for a jurisdiction. In the subsequent walkabout, Prince Philip endeavoured to demonstrate his knowledge of local history and quipped to an onlooker: 'I suppose you're an old soke.' The bystander took offence. No so well informed as the prince, he assumed that Philip was calling him a drunk.

At a garden party for eight thousand guests on the grounds of Buckingham Palace, Prince Philip was told by a guest that she was expecting her second child. 'I hope you can afford your hat,' he replied. A farmer then told him about the continental breeds of cattle he was rearing. Ever distrustful of anything foreign, the prince said: 'Oh, that awful tasting thing.'

At a show at Waltham Forest College in 2002 illustrating the changing fashions in the fifty years since the Queen had come to the throne, Prince Philip told model Somanah Achadoo: 'Your hair's too long, you should have had it cut for the Fifties.' Plainly he mistook the twenty-eight-year-old college lecture for a Royal Navy recruit.

On a visit to caves in Australia, he was told beware of the drips, to which he said: 'Oh I've run into plenty in my life.'

At a garden party in July 2003, Prince Philip was introduced to a perfectly respectable building boss who told him that he was retiring after years in a business renowned for cowboy operators. The prince only asked him whether or not he had any friends left.

At the ceremony in Normandy to commemorate the sixtieth anniversary of the D-Day landings, veteran Tom Gilhooley found himself standing on parade for over an hour. Prince Philip said to him: 'You're going to pay for it standing out in the sun for such a long time.' Later, the prince passed by again. By this time Tom's face was bright red and burning. 'I told you you'd pay for it standing out in the sun!' said Philip. 'We all had a good laugh,' said Gilhooley, happy that the prince had taken notice and remembered them.

On a trip to Malta in 2007, the prince asked a soon-to-be-wed couple in their thirties: 'How long have you been at it?' Just what he meant by this could not be ascertained.

At the Royal British Legion's Festival of Remembrance at the Albert Hall in 2007, the prince was reminded that, at the previous year's event, he had described the members of the association who had attended as mainly 'taxi drivers and clothing manufacturers.' The prince corrected him, saying: 'No, I said they were mainly taxi drivers and tailors.'

Water was a problem around Hull in 2008, when many people were forced from their homes by tidal flooding. Bidding farewell to the local council leader Carl Minns, the prince cleverly advised him to 'keep your head above water.'

Visiting the D-Day Museum in Portsmouth in 2009, the Duke of Edinburgh asked a woman what she did in the war. She replied that she was born in 1954, a full nine years after the war was over. (The confusion arose because fifty-five-year-old Linda Rivers was accompanying her eight-three-year-old mother Ena Davies, who was a veteran of the Land Army).

Visiting the town of Crawley, West Sussex, to mark its sixtieth anniversary, Prince Philip asked Claire Burns, the manager of Druckers Vienna Patisserie if she was responsible for making the people of Crawley overweight.

Moving on to the Thomas Bennett Community College, the prince popped his head around the door of the library and asked the teacher invigilating: 'Can they all read?'

Meeting a volunteer working for the Samaritans, the prince asked: 'You didn't try to commit suicide, did you?'

Stupidity

The prince is always ready for a stiff put-down to any question he considers stupid. In 2000, an official greeting him at a Canadian airport asked innocently: 'What was your flight like, Your Royal Highness?' Philip: 'Have you ever flown in a plane?' The official said: 'Oh yes, sir, many times.' 'Well,' said Philip, 'it was just like that.'

In 1997, the prince arrived at Cambridge University's Homerton College to open a new teaching block when he was approached by sixty-five-year-old car-park attendant Bob Proudfoot, who asked for his ticket. 'You bloody silly fool, I'm expected,' replied the prince before driving off, leaving Mr Proudfoot bemused. 'This chap flew into the car park driving a Land-Rover,' he said. 'I didn't expect it to be the Duke of Edinburgh, who was guest of honour of the college. I thought he would turn up in a big chauffeur-driven car... There was no reason to talk like that.'

The prince once berated a junior officer for being improperly dressed for dinner, but received some of his own sass back. 'What's that ordinary white shirt in aid of?' he asked. 'You're supposed to be wearing a dress shirt, aren't you?' To which the officer replied: 'I only wear that on special occasions.'

Visiting Bolton, Prince Philip was greeted by a city dignitary. 'Are you the town clerk?' asked the prince. Sean Harriss replied that he was the chief executive. 'Ridiculous title,' said the prince, who then wanted to know where Mr Harriss' ceremonial wig was. The harassed chief executive explained that he had left it in his office. 'It is something I will remember for the rest of my life,' said Harriss. 'He is famous for his sense of humour, so it is great to have shared a joke with him.'

When Calgary presented Prince Philip with his third Stetson – its version of giving a distinguished visitor the keys to the city – he remarked that he did not know what to do with it, other than to carry water or plant flowers in it. The Mayor of Calgary is said to have got his own back for what he considered to be a slight. Later when presenting the prince with some antlers, he told him: 'Don't ask me what to do with them, and I won't tell you where to stick them.'

The Arts

Replying to a toast at a British Film Academy dinner in 1958, he said: 'I warn you, this is going to be rather like one or two film premières that I've been to – you're going to discover that the introductory item will have turned out to be much more amusing and interesting than the main feature.'

Two years later, as president of the Society of Film and Television Art, he was presenting the awards at the BFA dinner and said: 'I thought it would be a good idea to come along and keep my eye on things.

I haven't been disappointed either as I have already noticed several very nice things to keep my eye on.'

On the Job

Prince Philip had trouble opening the Animal Health Trust's Farm in Essex in 1957. 'Ladies and gentlemen, it gives me the greatest pleasure to declare this laboratory open,' he announced, with one reasonable request: '... and if someone will lend me a key I will unlock it.'

In September 1964, when Prince Philip was to make a speech at the opening of the parliament of the newly-independent Malta, opposition leader Dom Mintoff threatened to walk out. In the event, Mintoff did not even turn up, but as the prince stepped onto the dais, the sergeant at arms signalled for everyone to stand. Philip said afterwards: 'For a moment I thought the whole audience was going to walk out on me!' (Which they did, in fact, seven years later, when Mintoff won the election and Malta became a republic).

In Australia in 1965, Prince Philip was asked what he had done at the two previous conferences for future industrial and community leaders in Oxford and Montreal. 'I flitted about, went to all the drinking parties, and rang a little bell sometimes.'

At the Defence Academy in Shrivenham, the prince was shown a grenade with a mini-parachute in the tail. After examining it closely, he said: 'I thought Heath Robinson was dead.' Prince Philip was asked to unveil a plaque he remarked casually: 'You are about to see the world's second-most experienced plaque-unveiler at work.'

As president of the Royal Mint Advisory Committee, Prince Philip vetoed the design of the new 50p coin in 1972, claiming 'I don't like that little "p."' The 'p' was replaced with the word 'pence.'

At a Master Tailors' Benevolent Association Banquet, he said: 'Your president has said that the royal family have a great beneficial effect on your trade, and what we wear today, you wear tomorrow – I hope there will be enough to go round.'

Industry & Science

Prince Philip has kept most of his more scathing remarks for Britain's captains of industry who he believe had let the country down in the 60s and 70s. Among the most moderate of his comments was the 1967 declaration: 'I'm sick of making excuses for this country.' Ten years later, obviously unimpressed with the way things were going, he made it clear he was prepared for the worst: 'Third World here we come.'

Industry

The problem with industry? 'There are too many one-ulcer men holding' two-ulcer jobs.' The prince himself maybe dyspeptic, but has never been know to suffer from ulcers. Indeed, he was proofed against them. His secret to staying ulcer-free? 'I think a sense of humour is almost vital for anybody nowadays, if you don't want to end up with ulcers.'

In 1948, it was suggested that he spend a month working as down a coal mine to bring him closer to the British people. But he could claim some experience already – visiting a Welsh steelworks in

May 1962, he pressed the button to start a new blast furnace. Then he signed the work sheet: 'Philip – turbine driver – 6 to 2 shift.'

'Occasionally I get fed up, going to visit a factory, when I am being shown around by the chairman, who clearly hasn't got a clue,' Prince Philip said, 'and I try to get hold of the factory manager but I can't because the chairman wants to make sure he's the one in all the photographs.'

Philip sums up industrialism fairly accurately: 'If anyone has a new idea in this country, there are twice as many people who advocate putting a man with a red flag in front of it.'

At a luncheon of the National Union of Manufacturers, the prince expressed his views on management: 'Many managerial problems seem to have perfectly simple and quite reasonable solutions, but if they fail to take the cussedness of man into account these are a waste of time.'

He also put modern technical advances into perspective: 'It is no good for man to seek to escape in luniks and rocketry and leave his soul morally earthbound among the television sets and expresso bars.' But Britain need not despair: 'We are certainly not a nation of nitwits. In fact, wits are our greatest single asset.'

'Sacred cows are all right in some pastures but they should not be welcomed in the fields of industry and commerce,' he said.

Considering the plight of those amateur mechanics who had to fix their own cars, he said at the opening of the Motor Show in 1953: 'As far as the owner-maintainer is concerned, beauty of line wears off very rapidly when he finds he can reach no part of the engine without standing on his head.' He also took a swing at the interior design: 'I am not always convinced that the driver's comfort is given enough thought. Why is it, for instance, that there is always a handle or a knob just opposite one's right knee? It may be, of course, that one should check that one is the same shape and size as the man who tested the car, but that many not always be possible.'

In 1956, he told the Society of Motor Manufacturers and Traders: 'I hope your products don't make as much smoke as you do.' He had more advice for motor manufacturers. As president of the Automobile Association, he suggested that the makers of diesel vehicles design their exhausts to send the fumes upwards. 'If it goes upwards, there is a chance of it being dispersed before it comes down and asphyxiates all the dogs and cats,' he said. 'I am sure diesel smoke is shortening my life.'

Never one to turn down an opportunity to tease with a pun, the prince once greeted the chairman of a textile group specializing in the production of knitting machines as the 'head knit.'

At a display of laundry equipment he asked: 'Which is the shrinking machine?'

At the annual dinner of the Institute of Fuel, guests were puffing on postprandial cigars, which provoked the prince to comment: 'It makes a rather splendid picture to see the members of the Institute of Fuel smoking like the proverbial chimneys.'

The Duke of Edinburgh said to a group of industrialists in 1961: 'I've never been noticeably reticent about talking on subjects about which I know nothing.' He later added: 'I am sure many of you have noticed that there is no better way of finding out about a subject than having to speak about it.'

In 1964, the Duke of Edinburgh told a meeting of aircraft experts that British safety standards are lower than those of several other countries. But he conceded: 'Airline operation is a hideously complicated business. The passenger is subject to ruthless statistical surgery.'

He told the Coal Board: 'How much longer can we

go on exploiting every feature of this country purely for gain?'

And he told the Electricity Board, when it claimed that it wasn't damaging the countryside as much as it had been damaged in the eighteenth century: 'Previous mistakes are not an excuse for making them again.'

Then again, he conceded: 'Anyone can start an argument at any time just by mentioning British railways or British roads.'

At a dinner to mark his eighty-seventh birthday in 2008, Prince Philip did his best Lord Browne at ease when he found himself sitting next to the former BP chief after a scandal concerning the disgraced peer's gay partner. 'I gather you've had some problems since we last met,' the prince told John Browne. 'Don't worry, there's a lot of that in my family,' he continued.

Unemployment

In the 1960s the prince was concerned about the society's pervasive laziness, which seemed to have taken as is mascot the perennially unemployed working-class cartoon figure Andy Capp. 'I dare say there will always be a certain number of Andy Capps in the community,' he said. 'But more leisure, education, mobility and money are going to make matters worse in a few years.'

On the rate of unemployment, the prince offers a little perspective: 'A few years ago, everybody was saying we must have more leisure, everyone's working too much,' he said. 'Now everybody's got more leisure time they're complaining they're unemployed. People don't seem to make up their minds what they want.' This was at the height of the 1981 recession.

A keen politician, the prince sees a smart way around the issue: 'Everybody talks about the unemployed. We would do much better to talk about the number of people who are employed because there are more of them.'

Science

In an address on the British Association for the Advancement of Science given to the Indian Science Congress in New Delhi, he said: 'I regret to say that my only degrees are honorary ones, a fact that will become only too apparent during my address about the British Association. The list of presidents alone reads like a telephone directory in the Hall of Fame; that is, of course, if you leave out a few names like mine, which are only conspicuous because they are so incongruous.'

73

Prince Philip told the Institute of Chemical Engineers that, since he had succeeded the distinguish physicist Sir Harold Hartley as president of the British Association for the Advancement of Science, it had gone 'from the sublime to the goblimey'.

In February 1958, he found himself address an audience of distinguished scientists at the annual luncheon of the Parliamentary and Scientific Committee. 'Once again, I find myself in a company of guests, each of whom is more qualified to speak than I am,' he said. 'There was a time when that sort of thing worried me, but I have since found that people like your guests are very long-suffering. Some of them, I suspect, are so delighted to be let off speaking themselves that they are prepared to put up with anything.'

Addressing scientists and engineers at a luncheon in Toronto in June 1959, he said: 'I would like to say how much I appreciate your invitation to address you today. I must add though, that it would be more appropriate for you to address me. Every now and then I get invitations of this sort and while I consider them a great honour I always try and get out of them because of the difficulty of trying to concoct something sensible to say. At least you've got together and saved me from doing this five times over. The course between platitudes and controversy is a rocky one, as most people who speak in public soon find out.'

Opening the Man-Made Fibres Building Exhibition in Leeds, he pointed to his own thinning locks and said: 'I'm not very good at man-made fibres myself.'

Not one to be stuck in the past, Prince Philip addresses the complications of progress: 'Progress is undiscriminating. Progress gives us better medical science, but it also gives us better bombs. How do you relate computers with compassion?'

On one occasion Prince Philip halted an erudite explanation by an esteemed scientist with the words: 'That's all very well, but you still haven't found out what makes my bath water gurgle.' On another occasion, he said: 'Science has been glamorised so long people think it can do no wrong.'

In 1954, after watching a film about ultrasonics at London University, he said: 'I was most interested to learn that the X-ray goes in one ear and out of the other.' Nevertheless, three years later, he was awarded an honorary doctorate in science at Reading University.

Proud of his progress, he told the boys of Uppingham School in Rutland: 'Everybody has got to understand a little bit about science or he can't understand what the hell goes on around him. Unless you know something about science, you won't get into the House of Commons.' Plainly that was where the boys from this exclusive boarding school were bound, but where Philip himself was sadly debarred.

Travel

Over her long reign, the Queen has become the most travelled monarch in history. Prince Philip often travels with her and has made numerous trips on his own. While official duties often make trips burdensome for the Queen, the prince is delighted with these junkets. 'I am all for people travelling at other people's expense,' he said.

As a frequent traveller, the prince is grateful for modern advancements: 'If you travel as much as we do, you appreciate the improvements in aircraft design of less noise and more comfort – provided you don't travel in something called economy class, which sounds ghastly.'

On travelling in style: 'I usually change my trousers on the plane, otherwise I get out looking like a bag.'

When Concorde was withdrawn after a crash in Paris that killed all one hundred passengers and nine crew, Prince Philip told British Airways staff: 'I must be the only person in Britain glad to see the back of that plane.' On its approach to Heathrow Airport,

Concorde would fly noisily over Windsor Castle. Prince Philip's favourite joke is about the American tourist who asked why they built Windsor Castle so close to Heathrow.

The prince also sought the end of another noisy bane of modern living, saying in 1984: 'If I can persuade you to join me in this campaign, the disappearance of the helicopter is assured and then we shall all be able to hold our heads high – as we march steadily back towards the caves our ancestors so foolishly vacated such a long time ago.'

Prince Philip asks the pressing questions. At the headquarters of GB Airways near Gatwick Airport, he asked the aircrew: 'When you think about all the publicity about planes being dangerous to fly in I wonder – why aren't all of you dead?'

Waiting at Newcastle Airport for an airliner of the Queen's Flight in the uniform of a Field Marshal, Prince Philip stormed out onto the tarmac, bellowing: 'Where's my bloody plane?' The air traffic controller in the tower, who failed to recognise their royal passenger, yelled back: 'Get that bloke in uniform off the apron, he shouldn't be there.' Philip was politely informed that the plane was not there because he had arrived half an hour early.

At a press conference in Sao Paulo in 1968, the

Prince was asked about the American's Apollo programme that would put a man on the moon the following year. 'It seems to me that it's the best way of wasting money that I know of,' he said. 'I don't think investments on the moon pay a very high dividend.'

In 1991, he visited NASA's headquarters in Houston, Texas, where he sat in the command seat of a space capsule simulator, which he then had to dock. 'It was like a bloody great mechanical copulator,' he said.

Prince Philip was stopped for speeding through Central London on 19 November 1947. 'I'm sorry officer,' he said, 'but I've got an appointment with the Archbishop of Canterbury.' He married Princess Elizabeth the next day and was on the way to a final rehearsal of the royal wedding.

On a tour of cruise liner *Queen Mary II* in 2004, Prince Philip was shown the ship's hospital. Senior medical officer Dr. Martin Carroll explained that about four people die on Cunard liners each year as they often carry terminally-ill passengers who had decided to live out their final days in luxury. When in the mortuary fridge, said the prince: 'So they book one of these in advance, eh?'
On the ship's twenty-one bars: 'You could have one big pub crawl,' he told purser Claudette Kirkwood.

In 1956, Prince Philip got the idea of visiting the Transantarctic Expedition, either at its base on the Ross Sea or the one on the Weddell Sea. Then it occurred to him that this would not be like one of his normal visits to one of the sunnier parts of the Commonwealth. 'I had to drop the idea in the end because it involved the risk of getting stuck there for fifteen months when I felt that my nuisance value would be out of all proportion,' he told the Antarctic Symposium in Melbourne.

At the annual dinner of the British Schools Exploring Society in April 1958, he addressed Sir Raymond Priestley, who was in the chair: 'Some forty years ago he spent, entirely unintentionally, the whole Antarctic Winter in an ice-cave with Commander Murray Levick and four others. Last year, he spent two months on *Britannia* with me. I'm not sure which experience he found more nerve-racking.'

In February 1957, Prince Philip had just returned from a world tour. He addressed a luncheon at the Mansion House, telling them of his travels: 'I find it difficult to realise that I have been round the world and covered nearly 40,000 miles since the fifteenth of October last year. It would be quite easy to claim that this journey was all part of a deep-laid scheme, but I am afraid I have to admit that it all came about because I was asked to start off the Olympics Games in Melbourne. In fact, it would have been much simpler to have flown out and flown back...'

When making a short TV film about driving on the newly introduced motorways, he said: 'Forgive me if I don't give examples of the wrong things which have been done, because that is sticking my neck out further than I usually do, and I don't want to get into any more trouble than necessary.'

When he was asked if there were countries he hadn't been to that he would like to visit. 'If I name them,' he said, 'they might invite me and then, if I couldn't make it, there'd be trouble.'

In 1962, ITV gave over forty-five minutes of air time to his South American tour. Out of deference to the prince they decided to run the show without any commercial breaks. However, at one point, he lost his thread. In an effort to regain his composure, he said: 'This seems like a natural break. I wonder if I could do a spot of advertising? Would that be right?'

That year, Prince Philip also published *Birds from Britannia*, an account of his visits to remote parts of the world during his world tours in 1956 and 1959. He began with an apologia: 'The photographs are in black and white simply because I prefer taking photographs in black and white. Fortunately most of the birds themselves are black and white, or grey anyway, so not much is lost.' The following years, he noted: 'I have had two books of speeches published, and one on birds. Needless to say, the one on birds was more successful.'

Lady Folk

Prince Philip has always had a keen eye for the ladies and the Queen often smiles when he makes straight for the prettiest young woman in the audience. 'He's a sailor at heart and a red-blooded male. I think she's still rather proud she snared him,' said a royal correspondent.

Prince Philip's cousin Alexandra, Queen of Yugoslavia, said: 'Blondes, brunettes and redhead charmers, Philip gallantly and, I think impartially, squired them all.' Indeed, assessing the courtiers' initial estimation of Lieutenant Philip Mountbatten as a potential spouse of the heir to the throne, the King's private secretary Sir Alan Lascelles wrote: 'They felt he was rough, uneducated and would probably not be faithful.'

After the 2003 Royal Variety Show he told thirty-year-old musician and TV presenter Myleene Klass in the line-up: 'You're fit aren't you.' 'I fell about laughing,' she said.

Four years later, he was introduced to Russell Brand and said about the young woman standing next to him: 'She's got all the right stuff in all the right places.' Apparently, Brand had not noticed.

Philip got lucky with Alesha Dixon, then with Mis-Teeq, in 2002. The R&B singer had been invited to sing at Buckingham Palace for the Jubilee concert where the Prince's attention was caught by her skimpy outfit. 'Aren't you cold, my dear?' he asked. She could not resist flirting. 'What are you going to do?' she replied. 'Lend me your jacket?'

Then in his sixties, Prince Philip was bowled over by the wife of the general manager to Compaq Computers. He had been invited to lunch by the chairman of Compaq, Ben Rosen. He asked an equerry for some tips on suitable topics of the conversation and was told of the prince's interest in aircraft, so Rosen took time out to mug up the BAe 146, a British-made four-engine jet. 'The prince and I were seated at the same table, separated by the wife of our UK general manager,' said Rosen. 'But from the moment we were seated, the prince spoke exclusively with the general manager's wife; neither I nor anyone else at the table could get a word in edgewise.

And I was the host! So it went during the appetiser dish and through the main course. Then, just as the waiters were clearing the entrée dishes, an opportunity presented itself. There was a momentary break in the conversation, and I seized the moment.

My opening line: "Your Royal Highness, I understand that you still fly airplanes.'"

Prince Philip broke off his conversation with the general manager's wife and fell momentarily silent. Then, with a withering look directed at Rosen, he said: 'Yes, you know, I am in that still period of life. That period when I can still lift a fork.'

He demonstrated lifting a fork.

'That period when I can still lift a glass.'

He lifted a glass.

'That period when I can still breathe.

He demonstrated breathing. Then there was a pause.

'Yes, I still fly.'

With that, he turned away from Rosen and returned to his conversation with the general manager's wife.

In 2010, pointing to a tartan tie being worn by Scottish Labour leader Iain Gray, the prince said to Scottish Tory leader Annabel Goldie: 'That's a nice tie. Are you wearing knickers made out of that material?' The doughty MSP quipped back: 'I couldn't possibly comment. And even if I had, I couldn't possibly exhibit them.' Overhearing the exchange were both the Queen and Pope Benedict XVI who was visiting Britain at the time.

Even at the age of ninety-one, the Prince had not lost his eye for a pretty woman. During the Queen's

Diamond Jubilee tour in 2012, he spotted a twenty-five-year-old blonde council worker who was wearing an eye-catching red dress with a zip running down the front, and whispered to a nearby police: 'I would get arrested if I unzipped that dress.' The policeman struggled to stifle his laughter.

Prince Philip seems to have a preoccupation with the ladies' fasteners. During a private view of jewellery designed by award-winning silversmith Jocelyn Burton at Bentley & Skinner in Piccadilly later that year, he spoke up for all spouses when he complained of the problem of undoing jewellery fastenings. 'Those infernal clasps are absolutely impossible. You fiddle with them for hours, then they suddenly come undone and they fall on the floor but you have no idea why. When you try to close them again you find you just can't do it.'

At a cocktail party to support the World Wide Fund for Nature, Prince Philip pounced on fashion writer Serena French. 'I suppose you'll be looking out for people wearing mink coats then,' he said. 'Surely nobody would wear fur to a wildlife fund event,' said another guest. 'Well, you never know what they're wearing underneath,' said the prince. Turning back to Ms French, he added: 'You're not wearing mink knickers are you?' Then he roared with laughter.

Spotting a twelve-year-old girl in Aberdeen in 2012

who was wearing a 'Kickers' jumper, he said: 'I thought that said Knickers.'

Prince Philip is certainly old-school when it comes to women's liberation. At a drinks party at Buckingham Palace in 2000, he spotted a group of female Labour MPs who name badges were clear prefixed 'Ms'. 'Ah, so this is feminist corner then,' he said. The MPs merely burst out laughing. One said: 'I was not offended. It was clearly meant as a joke.' Another said: 'We thought it was hilariously funny that he assumed a group of Labour women must be raving feminists.' But then in 1987, he had said to a woman solicitor: 'I thought it was against the law for a woman to solicit.'

In 2009, he asked a women's group in Hull: 'Still downtrodden then?'

Visiting Lambeth Palace with the Queen in 2012, he was passing an area in front of the press pit – itself predominately female – where a number of women, including a nun and the Reverend Canon Dr Frances Ward, the Dean of St Edmundsbury Cathedral, were sitting. 'So this is the female section,' he said. 'Are you all gathered here for protection?' In Kenya in 1984, when a local lady gave him a figurine as a gift, he said: 'You are a woman aren't you?'

In San Francisco in 1983, he met mayor Dianne

Feinstein and several female members of the city council and remarked: 'Aren't there any male officials? This is a nanny city.'

Meeting four belly dancers in their forties in Swansea, he said: 'I thought Eastern women just sit around smoking pipes and eating sweets all day.' One of them, forty-seven-year-old Beverly Richards, replied: 'We do that as well.' 'I can see that,' said the prince with a glint in his eye.' Later Beverly said: 'We were stunned, then burst out laughing. But it's an honour to be insulted by royalty. It's something to tell the grandchildren.' She admitted they were a little overweight, but said: 'We are certainly full of Eastern promise.'

Afterwards, the prince watched a demonstration of surfing by Chris Griffiths. When he explained he was a professional surfer, Prince Philip said: 'Good god! You mean somebody paid you to do that.'

Visiting Wyven Barracks in Exeter in 2010, he asked twenty-four-year-old sea cadet Elizabeth Rendle what she did for a living. When she told him she worked in nightclub. He asked: 'Oh, what, a strip club?' When she said no, he thought better of it, saying it was 'probably too cold for that anyway'.

One can only speculate what was on Prince Philip's mind in 2000 when he saw robots bumping into each other and said: 'They're not mating are they?'

When journalist Fiammetta Rocco interviewed him for the *Independent on Sunday* in 1992, she noticed that had a copy of a book called *Sex In Our Time* among the volumes on naval history on the bookshelves in his office. She also asked him about extra-marital affairs. (His name has been linked with Daphne du Maurier, whose husband worked in his private office; the cabaret star Helene Cordet and actress Anna Massey. Over the years, his name was also linked to those of glamorous television personality Katie Boyle, film star Merle Oberon and Princess Alexandra.) Asked by Fiammetta Rocco about the rumoured affairs, he said: 'Good God woman, I don't know what sort of company you keep. Have you ever stopped to think that for the last forty years I have never moved anywhere without a policeman accompanying me? So how the hell could I get away with anything like that?'

Despite the rumours and his womanizing tendencies, there is no question of the Prince's loyalty to the Queen: 'How could I be unfaithful to the Queen? There is no way that she could possibly retaliate.' On another occasion he said: 'My job, first, second and last is never to let the Queen down.'

In 1956 when Philip took off on world tour by himself, leaving his wife and young family behind, the headline: 'Report – Queen, Duke in rift over party girl,' appeared in the *Baltimore Sun*. 'Not since the first rumours of a romance between the former King Edward VIII and the then-Mrs Simpson have Americans gobbled up the London dispatches so avidly,' commented journalist Alistair Cooke.

In 1948, just a year after he was married, Prince Philip had met showgirl Pat Kirkwood, whose legs were once described by critic Kenneth Tynan as 'the eighth wonder of the world.' On rumours of their presumed affair, true to royal tradition, Prince Philip remained unswervingly silent.

In 2010, he flirted with Carla Bruni when she visited Windsor with her husband President Nicolas Sarkozy. He also made a beeline for Qatari beauty Sheikha Mozah when she visited Windsor with her husband the Emir. The prince showed her artefacts from the Queen's first visit to the Gulf, saying: 'That was 1979, you weren't born then?' 'Yes, I wasn't born then,' she replied with in twinkle. Not only had seen been born, she was already twenty and married to the Emir.

His carriage driving partner Lady Penny Romsey, an attractive aristocrat thirty years his junior, also gave rise to fevered speculation. One morning, they were out for a spin on Holkham beach when they came across nudists. The prince simply raised his hat and said: 'Good morning.'

At eighty-five, he told Jeremy Paxman: 'As far as I'm concerned, every time I talk to a woman, they say I've been to bed with her – as if she had no say in the matter. Well, I'm bloody flattered at my age to think some pretty girl is interested in me. It's absolutely cuckoo.' Years before, he told Patricia Brabourne, Lord Mountbatten's daughter: 'The way papers write about my affairs I might as well have done it.'

In 1988, Prince Philip famously remarked: 'When a man opens the car door for his wife, it's either a new car or a new wife.'

In Canada, Prince Philip was introduced to author Carol Shields and asked her what she wrote about. 'I write about women and their problems,' she replied. This was too much for the prince. 'What about men and their problems?' he said. Then after a stony silence, Philip back-pedalled. 'On second thoughts,' he said, 'there isn't much to say. They've only got one problem and that's women.'

In the early 1970s, the Queen, Prince Philip and their four children spent their holidays in Ross-shire, where they met Rob Tweddle, a naturalist at the Inverpolly Nature Reserve. Tweddle recalled: 'One day I was driving along a little narrow road with Philip in the car and we came across a green Morris Minor that had run off of the road. The offside wheels had gone into a ditch. Two female teachers were standing at the side of the road. I stopped the car and Philip jumped out and we actually lifted the car back on to the road. Philip said to them 'now don't do that again' and we got back in the car. When I looked back they were still standing with their mouths open.' At the very least, it can be said that Philip has a knack for impressing women.

Arts and Entertainment

Asked at a Foreign Press Association lunch in 1964 whether he thought the royal family was interested in the arts, Prince Philip said: 'There is no art form in this country that has not go some member of the royal family at the head of it.... We live in what virtually amounts to a museum.'

However, Prince Philip does show some discernment when it comes to the arts. After being told that Madonna was singing the James Bond Die Another Day theme in 2002, Prince Philip said: 'Are we going to need ear plugs?' He was not alone in this opinion. Grammy award winning composer David Arnold, a veteran of the last three Bond movies, described her synthesised, techno dance track as 'the worst Bond song ever'. He also expressed sympathy for the prince who attended the premier. 'I felt sorry for the old boy having to sit through that – it was very loud,' he said. As to the ear plugs? 'If I'd had a pair, I would have given him them.'

The prince also had little time for loud music. He told a group of children from the British Deaf

Association standing close to a steel band at a Prince's Trust event at Cardiff Castle in 2000: 'Deaf? If you're near that music, it's no wonder you are deaf.'

After tenor Russell Watson finished a cutlery-rattling rendition of Jerusalem at the dinner at Buckingham Palace in 2011, Prince Philip said: 'That was magnificent, but why do you need a bloody microphone? They could have heard you in outer space.' Then he turned to singer's partner Louise Harris and said: 'You must go deaf listening to him all the time.' Indeed for his ninetieth birthday, the Royal National Institute for the Deaf gave the prince a pair of ear defenders – to use when he goes shooting. 'Can you get Radio Three on them?' he asked when they were presented to him.

Other singers also came in for some flak. After the Royal Variety Show in 1969, Prince Philip asked Tom Jones: 'What do you gargle with – pebbles?' He added the following day: 'It is very difficult at all to see how it is possible to become immensely valuable by singing what I think are the most hideous songs.' He took another swing at the Welsh singer at a small-business lunch discussing how difficult it is to get rich in Britain, saying: 'What about Tom Jones? He's made a million and he's a bloody awful singer.'

Prince Philip also described Adam Faith's voice as sounding like bath water going down the plug hole.

Then in 2006 he asked the petite Welsh opera singer Katherine Jenkins: 'How are your vocal chords?' 'Fine thank you,' she replied. 'No boils or warts on them yet,' the concerned Prince said.

Not that Prince Philip does not rate singers above other show-business celebrities. After Piers Morgan introduced *Britain's Got Talent* winner, tenor Paul Potts, to the royal couple, Prince Philip asked: 'You're judges, is that right?' Morgan, who was accompanied by Simon Cowell and Amanda Holden, said they were. 'So,' chuckled the prince, looking back at Cowell before pointing to Paul Potts, 'you sponge off him then?' Prince Philip insisted that he did not know enough about Simon Cowell to insult him, but Piers Morgan was adamant. 'I can categorically say it happened,' he said.

In 2012, Prince Philip showed some concern for the Canadian quartet The Tenors who gave a performance at Windsor Castle for the Diamond Jubilee. Before the show, he said: 'I hope your voices don't break in the show.' They were all in their twenties.

At his seventieth birthday party at Windsor Castle, Prince Philip was introduced to Terrie Doherty, head of Sony Music Regional Promotion in London. 'God,' he said. 'Do you have to speak to those awful DJ chappies?'

At a medieval fayre in Old Windsor, a young woman in costume had found a quiet corner to breast-feed her baby. Prince Philip spotted her and announced loudly: 'Oh look everyone, she really taken the part to heart. She's is breast feeding her child.'

Prince Philip is not a man to be starstruck. When Oscar-winning actress Cate Blanchett told him that she worked 'in the film industry,' he asked her whether she could fix his DVD player, saying: 'There's a cord sticking out of the back. Might you tell me where it goes?' After Cate explained that this was really not her province as she was an actress, he 'seemed a bit non-plussed.' Miss. Blanchett has played Elizabeth I on screen twice, though she has yet to play Elizabeth II.

If a DVD player was not puzzling enough, in 2001, he told students at Sussex University that he was equally non-plussed with the TV, saying he had to scrabble around on the floor with a torch and magnifying glass to find the switch to turn it on. 'The only thing you need to know is how to turn it on and they try and hide it from you,' he said. 'To work out how to operate a TV you practically have to make love to the thing,' he said in an interview celebrating the fiftieth anniversary of a Design Council prize in his name.

He also told Kevin McCloud, the presenter of Channel Four's *Grand Designs*, of his frustration with modern technology. 'They put the TV controls on the bottom so you had to lie on the floor,' he said, 'and then if you wanted to record something, the recorder was underneath, so you ended up lying on the floor with a torch in your teeth, a magnifying glass and an instruction book. Either that or you had to employ a grandson of age ten to do it for you.' He wanted to know 'why can't you have a handset that people who are not ten years old can actually read?' In addition to technological issues, he also railed against fascia panels in cars that were sometimes unreadable due to light reflection and complained about car fuel gauges that only told drivers how much fuel was left, not how much was needed to refill the tank.

After failing to recognise Australian actress Cate Blanchett, Prince Philip was no more cognisant of home-grown celebrities. On the set of the soap *EastEnders* set in 2001, he asked Adam Woodyatt who had played Ian Beale since the show started in 1985: 'Are you an actor or an operator?'

At the premiere of *The Chronicles of Narnia: The Voyage of the Dawn Treader* he asked Simon Pegg, who played talking mouse Reepicheep: 'When did you realise you had the voice of a mouse?'

Australian stand-up comedian and TV presenter

Adam Hills, who has a prosthetic limb, was told: 'You could smuggle a bottle of gin out of the country in that artificial foot.'

It seems that the Duke of Edinburgh was no fan of *Poirot* either. When lunching with the Queen and Prince Philip, David Suchet was confronted with a mango, but had no idea of how to peel it in polite company, so he turned to the Duke for advance. 'You don't peel a mango, you slice it,' blustered the Prince, grabbing a knife to demonstrate. The so-called 'mango incident' found its way into the series. In the episode 'The Royal Ruby,' a fellow diner asks Poirot how he had learned to deal with a mango. 'A certain duke taught me,' he says.

Shown his portrait by artist Stuart Pearson Wright, Prince Philip exclaimed: 'Gadzooks!' – a word that has not been in normal usage for nearly two hundred years. It means 'God's hooks,' that is, the nails that pinned Christ to the cross. Asked if the painting was a good likeness, the prince said: 'I bloody well hope not... As long as I don't have to have it on the wall.' He was depicted bare-chested with a fly on his shoulder and watercress sprouting from his index finger. 'Why have you given me a great schonk?' he demanded. The *Sunday Times* commented: 'Uncanny, isn't it, that when you paint a picture of Prince Philip, the insults just seem to follow you around the room?'

The *Daily Telegraph* pointed out that the word 'schonk' – presumably meaning nose – was a new coinage. It seems to be a hybrid of 'schnozzle' and 'conk.' In the past, Prince Philip had been a 'trifle sniffy' where new words were concerned, the paper said. In 1982, he compiled a list for *Logophile* magazine of what he called his 'Fourteen Most Ugsome Words.' They were 1) Nihilism 2) Macho 3) Charismatic 4) Pseudo- 5) Audio- 6) Socio- 7) Upcoming 8) Avant-garde 9) Conurbation 10) Camp 11) Obscene 12) Gay 13) Logophile 14) Imperialism 'These are parasitic words,' he explained. 'They make no sense on their own and don't improve the words to which they are added.'

The prince did not have much better luck with artist John Orr RA, who was painting his official portrait as president of the Naval and Military Club. He told Orr that, in the days of empire, cannibals got mad cow disease, but 'it just disappeared when they stopped eating each other.'

At the Royal Variety Performance in Blackpool in 2009, Prince Philip asked the eleven members of the multi-ethnic dance troupe Diversity at the 2009 Royal Variety Performance: 'Are you all one family?' Obviously not, Prince Philip compounded the folly by then asking the troupe: 'Did you all come over just for this show?' 'I thought, no they're from London,' said comic Jason Manford. 'They've done the same journey you have.'

When Prince Philip sat in the royal box with the Queen at the Royal Variety Show watching the stripping scene from The Full Monty, he turned to biographer Gyles Brandreth and said: 'Don't worry, she's been to Papua New Guinea and seen it all before.'

Backstage at the Adelphi Theatre in London, chorus girls from the hit show *Chicago* clad in fishnet stockings, high heels, skimpy shorts and bra tops flocked around the prince. 'Where on earth do you keep your microphones?' he asked. The hoofers told him that their radio mics were hidden in their hair.

When Elton John told near-neighbour Prince Philip in 2001 that he had sold his gold Aston Martin, the prince replied: 'Oh, it's you that owns that ghastly car – we often see it when driving to Windsor Castle.' But then, he was never a great fan of Elton John. In 2001, at the Seventy-third Royal Variety Show, Elton performed three songs with his back to the royal box. The Queen said: 'I wish he would turn the microphone to one side.' Prince Philip said: 'I wish he'd turn the microphone off!' Again the prince proved himself a bastion of good sense.

Architecture

Prince Philip plainly shares some of his son Prince Charles' conservative views on architecture. Reviewing the plans for the twelve-bedroom mansion Prince Andrew, Duke of York, shared with his wife Sarah Ferguson at Sunninghill Park, he said: 'It looks like a tart's bedroom.' The press then dubbed it South York after South Fork, the ranch house in the TV soap *Dallas*. After the break-up of Prince Andrew's marriage, the mansion was sold to Kazakh businessman Timur Kulibayev for more than £3 million above the asking price of £12 million and was then left to rot.

Prince Philip told residents of tower blocks that they would be better off if their flats were pulled down, though that would render them homeless.

In 1958, he told architects in Scotland: 'I think is worth remembering, when you look around, that everything that has not been made by God, has probably been perpetrated by an architect.' And he had come up with an ingenious way of spotting the guilty men at a distance: 'All architects wear ties with horizontal strips... or no ties at all.'

He had another go at architects in Ghana the following year. Addressing a luncheon during a state visit there, he said: 'If I attempted to visit or have lunch with all the institutions, associations and groups which are involved in the development of

Ghana at this particularly important moment in her history, I would have to stay here very much longer. Therefore, I am very pleased that the surveyors, engineers and architects have all got together today to arrange this very pleasant function. It has allowed me to hit three professional bodies with one brick, which is a much more interesting occupation than throwing stones at birds.'

At luncheon at the Modular Society in 1962, he said: 'Without wishing to be rude in any way, anything which encourages architects to occasionally break away from the cigar box and gasometer-line ought to be encouraged.'

Noting that a large new building had recently replaced what had used to be a brewery, he said: 'I am not quite sure which is worse, the sight which is there now, or the smell which used to be there.'

MP Chris Mullin put his foot in it when visiting the new GCHQ building in Cheltenham with Prince Philip in 2004. 'Would Charles approve?' asked Mullin. 'Charles who?' the prince replied.

Having made himself the enemy of architects, Prince Philip endeared himself to accountants when he told a gag to the Association of Chartered Certified Accountants: 'Three accountants go for a job interview and are asked to add up two plus two. The first accountant thinks for a bit and says 'five.' The second punches the numbers into his calculator and comes up with 'four' while the third replies, "The answer can be whatever you want."' Ian Welch, head of corporate communications at ACCA, also noted: 'When he was introduced to our creative department he looked bemused – until it was explained that they handle things like the website rather than create figures.'

Prince Philip chaired a lecture at the Royal Society of Arts in 2004 about Prince Albert and his contribution to the Great Exhibition of 1851. During questions, one lady Fellow remarked: 'I understand that the Crystal Palace of the Great Exhibition appears to have been built on time. With the advances of modern technology, why can't we do the same today? The Millennium Dome had its problems, and, with great respect to your Royal Highness, the Athens Olympics seems destined to be seriously delayed.' Sticking up for his homeland, the prince piped up: 'It's Paris that has the problems not Greece – look at Charles de Gaulle Airport.'

The theatre

At a gala performance of Cameron Mackintosh's musical Betty Blue Eyes in aid of the Grenadier Guards – one of the regiments Prince Philip is colonel of – he saw himself and his wife portrayed on stage. Afterwards he told Annalisa Rossi, who played the Queen: 'You remind me of somebody...' Dan Burton played the prince as he had been sixty-four years earlier. While the Prince's hair was now thinning, he pointed to Burton's luxuriant wig and said: 'I like the hair.'

At the premiere of True Blue, a film funded by Channel Four, Prince Philip said to the channel's chairman Sir Michael Bishop: 'So you're responsible for the kind of crap Channel Four produces!' The prince then asked another executive what he did. The producer of True Blue replied: 'I commission the kind of crap you're going to see.'

After the Royal Variety Performance in 2003, Prince Philip said of the ever-youthful Donny Osmond: 'Will someone please give some grey hair to this kid?' Osmond was forty-five.

Praising the courage of an avant-garde artist, Prince Philip said: 'She had the courage to send in a pair of kippers to this year's Royal Academy Exhibition and have them hung.'

Food and Drink

For a man of simple tastes, Prince Philip complained about the rich food served up at state dinners. 'I never see any home cooking,' he said. 'All I get is fancy stuff.' Examining the French menu at one gala bash, he remarked sarcastically: 'Oh good, fish and chips again.'

The entertainment was up to much at state banquets either. After a particularly boring speech, he said to toast-master Ivor Spencer: 'At least you get paid for this.'

In 1964, he did conceded that 'British food is like a small child. When it's good it's very, very good' when it's bad, it's absolutely awful.' But, he rued in 2007: 'Lunches are seldom free.'

Tony Blair also recounted how during a weekend barbecue at Balmoral – 'a vivid combination of the intriguing, the surreal and the utterly freaky' – Prince Philip did the cooking while the Queen donned rubber gloves and washed the dishes. This might be due to the Prince's school of thought that, as he mentioned to the Scottish Women's Institute in1961, 'British women can't cook.'

The royal couple had problem with the thick icing on an elaborate fruit cake at the 250th anniversary of the opening of the Royal Botanic Gardens at Kew. The cake, which was shaped like Kew's famous Palm House and took sixty hours to bake was resistant to the Queen's cake knife, prompting Philip to shout: 'Cut it properly. Press down harder!' The Queen scowled at Philip before stepping aside and suggesting he take the knife. He then said: 'Let's just check if it really is a cake because sometimes they aren't.' Confirming that it was a real cake, he launched into a number of confectionary jokes.

Early on in their marriage, the royal couple had other problems with cake. They were crossing the water to Vancouver Island in Canada. The weather was unsettled and the ship was rocking violent. Just as a young petty officer arrived in the royal suite, the ship lurched and the tray of tea cakes he was holding crashed to the floor. The prince fell to his knees and helped to gather them up. After retrieving a handful of cakes, he returned to his seat. Turning to Princess Elizabeth he remarked, 'I've got mine – yours are down there.'

At the Royal Dairy Show in 1965, he said: 'None of the beef I have eaten at this age is edible.'

After competing in Hungary in 2004, he said: 'The most dangerous part of that tournament was visiting the Hungarian camp, because whatever the time of day, they gave you a glass of peach brandy and you were lucky to escape with your life.' The food was also a danger. He famously told a British visitor in Budapest in 1993: 'You can't have been here long – you haven't got a pot belly.'

On being offered the finest Italian wines to wash down the exquisite young goat and chestnut served up by Prime Minister Giuliano Amato at a dinner in Rome in 2000, Prince Philip declined, saying: 'Get me a beer. I don't care what kind it is, just get me a beer!' He pulled the same trick at banquet in Germany in 2004. 'Try the German wine, sir,' said a diplomat. 'It's from the most northern vineyard in the world.' Philip replied in German, saying only: 'I'll have a beer.'

He did not get on much better with French food. After award-winning French chef Regis Crépy provided a breakfast of bacon, eggs, smoked salmon, kedgeree, croissants and pain au chocolat at his floating pub Il Punto on the river Orwell at Ipswich, Prince Philip remarked: 'French cooking's all very well, but they can't do a decent English breakfast.' Perhaps the Prince was just sticking up for the full English and echoing novelist W. Somerset Maugham who said: 'To eat well in England, you should have a

107

breakfast three times a day.'

Invited to a luncheon in 1974, Philip said: 'It is a myth that I eat grilled journalists for breakfast.'

Offered some fish from Rick Stein's Seafood Deli, he said: 'No, I would probably end up spitting it out over everybody.' Employee Louise Atkinson said she was convinced that the Duke had not meant to insult her boss or his cooking. 'He was very interested in where our fish came from. Then he just came out with that remark. I think he meant it was rather crumbly and he was worried he would spray it over the next people he was going to meet,' she said.

At a dinner party in 2004, he said: 'Bugger the table plan, give me my dinner.' And he likes a tipple. When presented with a food hamper by the US ambassador to the court of St James, he asked: 'Where's the Southern Comfort?' However, he is sometimes not so tolerant when others are in their cups. On one occasion he snapped at the senior naval officers who had two martinis before lunch: 'Well admiral, what you think? – that is, if you're capable of thinking.'

Proposing a toast at the Land Agents' Society Jubilee Dinner in 1953, he said: 'First of all may I thank you very much indeed for a most excellent and enormous dinner. I cannot help thinking that if this is your usual standard, then I suggest that land agents should eat half as much and then we should not have to produce twice as much food... I was surprised to learn that it was only fifty years ago that you decided to get together. But, speaking as a landowner, or a part landowner, it is just as well to learn that you did not get together sooner.'

The Royal Society of Medicine had attained its 150th anniversary in 1964 and Prince Philip was invited to address their jubilee dinner. 'If I don't know anything about medicine, at least I can claim to be an expert on anniversary dinners,' he said. 'Nearly one hundred and fifty anniversary dinners – what a splendid thought. How many tons of food? How many gallons of wine? And how many hours of speeches have gone into your history? And how many cracks about "physician heal thyself" afterwards?'

At Bourke, New South Wales, Prince Philip visited a fruit farm. Commenting on the way the produce was packaged, he said: 'Oh, you're going in for this business of keeping people out of the food. No way can you open the bloody thing.' This came the day after a visit to a cheese factory in Wagga Wagga, where he ruined an entire day's production by refusing to wear sterile clothes.

As the Queen opened the Commonwealth heads of government meeting in Malta in 2005, the eighty-four-year-old Prince Philip was touring a food canning factory on its sister island of Gozo, wearing a hairnet over his thinning locks. Staff presented him with two specially prepared jars of spicy fruit, telling him they would send him two tins every year for the rest of his life. 'You won't have to do that for very long then,' the prince retorted. He then watched bottles of ketchup being labelled and packed. Spotting a worker wearing large, white gumboots, asked: 'What have you been doing – treading tomatoes?'

Lynwood Westray is the famous White House butler who served eight presidents over thirty-two years. When the Queen and Prince Philip visited President Jimmy Carter in 1979, Westray asked the prince: 'Your majesty, would you like a cordial?' Westray should, of course, have called him 'Your Royal Highness.' But this breathtaking breach of protocol paid dividends. Prince Philip said: 'I'll take one if you'll let me serve you.' Later, Westray said: 'Oh my God, this had never happened before. There we were standing there. I was holding the glasses and my buddy was holding the liqueurs and we looked at each other, and I said: 'If that's the only way you'll have it, we'll go along with it.' And the prince served us what he was having, and the three of us had a drink and a conversation. It was an honour to let him do it.'

All Creatures Great and Small

Although Prince Philip served as the president of the World Wildlife Fund from its founding in 1961, he has always been keen of field sports. Over his lifetime, he is estimated to have shot over 150,000 pheasants, usually those bred for the purpose on the royal estate at Sandringham. However, leading a shooting party in 2004, he made a slight miscalculation. They were shooting game near the edge of the estate, with the dead birds plummeting to the ground some twenty yards from the playground of a local school. The gundogs dutifully collected the carcasses, but the carnage left the young pupils in tears in what was considered by the tabloids as a gaffe – albeit a non-verbal one.

In 1957, long before he became president of the World Wildlife Fund, Prince Philip shot a crocodile in The Gambia. Two of the three species of crocodiles there are on the endangered species list. 'It's not a very big one, but at least it's dead and it took an awful lot of killing!'

Even when he went on to become president of the

World Wildlife Fund in 1981, he continued to defend his own interest in hunting. Comparing blood sports to a butcher killing animals to sell meat, in 1988 he said: 'I don't think doing it [killing animals] for money makes it any more moral. I don't think a prostitute is more moral than a wife, but they are doing the same thing. It is really rather like saying it is perfectly all right to commit adultery providing you don't enjoy it.'

Wading into the fox-hunting debate in 2004, Prince Philip said: 'Fox hunting is a curious thing to ban, because of all the blood sports it's the only one where the people following it don't come anywhere near a wild animal at all.'

At a project to protect turtle doves in Anguilla in 1965, Prince Philip courted controversy by saying: 'Cats kill far more birds than men. Why don't you have a slogan: "Kill a cat and save a bird?"' In 2008, he persisted in that view, saying: 'People don't like to admit it, but cats catch an enormous number of small wild birds. But people are very attached to their cats – it's a fact of life.' His view is supported by leading New Zealand economist and environmentalist Gareth Morgan who, in 2013, proposed that his homeland be made a cat-free country to preserve its wildlife.

Prince Philip also gave advice to a rabbit breeder on Anguilla in 1994: 'Don't feed your rabbits pawpaw fruit – it acts as a contraceptive. Then again, it might not work on rabbits.' He had an affection for the fruit. The villagers of Yaohnanen on Vanuatu believe that their god, Prince Philip, will return when the pawpaw is ripe. Instead he suggested the Anguillans eat, instead, their wild goats. 'You only need some idiot to let some rabbits escape and they will be all over the place,' he said.

Other creatures had reason to fear the president of the World Wildlife Fund. 'We have no intention of campaigning against mousetraps or flypapers,' the prince said.

On a tour of South Africa, Prince Philip found himself in an earnest discussion about the reluctance of pandas to breed in captive. One of the guests maintained that a panda in a zoo becomes too attached to its keeper. The prince chipped in: 'Well, then, the logical solution would seem to be to dress one of the pandas up as a zookeeper so that the other one fancies it.'

Celebrating the 550th anniversary of Magdalen College, Oxford, Prince Philip joined the dons for lunch. After consuming a main course of venison, the prince noticed Magdalen's much-prized herd of deer in the college grounds. 'How many of those buggers did you have to shoot for lunch, then?' he asked the bursar. Told no college deer had been slaughtered for the meal as their supply came from Kent, Philip quipped: 'Well, don't tell Charles because he likes everyone to buy local.'

Prince Philip also has forthright opinions on farming. He told *Shooting Times*: 'They are constantly trying to produce cattle that will produce more milk and less cow – like a hat-rack with an udder attached. They can't really go on making such a travesty of an animal, there must be a limit to this. Even more ridiculous is the fact that milk is actually cheaper than bottled water. It seems quite bizarre to me.'

When asked by a farming magazine if conservation were not too important to be left to conservationists, he said: 'I would say that farming is too important to be left to farmers.'

Prince Philips does not agree with Prince Charles over organic farming methods. 'Organic farming is not an absolute certainty that it's quite as useful as it sounds. You have got to be emotionally committed to it – but if you stand back and be open-minded about it, it is quite difficult to really find where it has been a real benefit.' His son, patron of the Soil Association, did not agree with him and suffered some ridicule when he introduced organic systems in Highgrove in the 1980s. 'It's interesting now that it isn't ridiculed to the same degree,' he said. 'I think people are beginning to realise that some of the chickens are coming home to roost and settle heavily in the genetically modified trees.'

More than once Prince Philip has expressed a wish that, if there was such a thing as reincarnation, he could come back as a deadly virus. This has been used to tar him as a misanthropist. However, he has provided good reasons for his wish. In a forword to *If I Were an Animal* by Fleur Cowles in 1987, the prince wrote: 'I just wonder what it would be like to be reincarnated in an animal whose species had been so reduced in numbers that it was in danger of extinction. What would be its feelings toward the human species whose population explosion had denied it somewhere to exist... I must confess that I am tempted to ask for reincarnation as a particularly deadly virus.' Then in 1988, he said: 'In the event that I am reincarnated, I would like to return as a deadly virus, to contribute something to solving overpopulation.' He believes that people should limit their families to two children, though he has four himself. The prince has declared himself against mass sterilisation though.

While Prince Philip was serious about conservation, 'I'm not green,' he told the BBC's Fiona Bruce. 'I'm not a bunnyhugger, one who simply loves animals. People are more concerned about how you treat a donkey in Sicily than conservation.'

As head of the World Wildlife Fund, Prince Philip often expressed his concern about the fate of the tropical rain forests of Southeast Asia and their denizens. After accepting a conservation award in Thailand in 1991, he levelled his sights as his hosts, saying: 'Your country is one of the most notorious centres of trading in endangered species.'

At a speech in New York in June 1962, he condemned African poachers for killing off rhinoceros to export their horns to China. 'For some incomprehensible reason, they seem to think it acts as an aphrodisiac,' he said. 'They might as well grind up chair legs.'

In his book *Men, Machines and Sacred Cows* Prince Philip discussed more fully his attitude to the horse: 'Some optimists tend to assume that once you have learned the lesson that horses bite at one end and kick at the other, there is nothing further to worry about. No such luck, I'm afraid. The horse is a great leveller and anyone who is concerned about his dignity would be well advised to keep away from horses. Apart from many other embarrassments there is, for instance, no more ridiculous sight than a horse performing its natural functions with someone in full dress uniform mounted on its back.' He has been there on several state occasions.

Prince Philip also said that lucky is the man who finds

himself in 'the ideal arrangement' of having a wife who can be persuaded to 'keep, groom and train their ponies.' Fortunately, the Queen is an ardent horsewoman.

At dinner on the night before Trooping of the Colour in 2006, when he was eighty-five, he was asked where he would be riding in the procession the following day. 'No, I'm not,' he said. 'The horse is too old.'

The Environment and Overpopulation

Prince Philip has fearlessly waded into the highly contentious issue of climate change, stressing the impact of population increase on the production of greenhouse gases. 'People go on about this carbon footprint,' he said, 'but they fail to realise that the amount of carbon going into the atmosphere is entirely dependent on the number of people living on the earth. There are now sixty million people living in this country and we are about the same land size as New Zealand – this country had three million people in Elizabeth I's day.' He added: 'I think that the greatest problem for the future is population growth. The population has quadrupled in my lifetime.' Prince Philip is not quite as old as he thinks he is. The population of Great Britain was around forty-three million when he was born in 1921.

In 1990, he gave a speech on the threat of overpopulation. Here, he attacks those who claim that the growth of the population in India was desirable because it had 'stimulated agricultural output... anyone who believes that we can somehow push people out to find a new home on some other planet or some other solar system can only be a science fiction addict.' In 1968, he advocated a 'tax on babies'.

Philip was for birth control to limit the number of children in a family, saying: 'You can't expect to go a on a bender and not expect a hangover.' Addressing the vexed problems of Thais using multi-coloured condoms, he said: 'They choose yellow if they are happy and black if they are in mourning.'

Japanese businessman Eishiro Saito, chairman of the Global Infrastructure Fund told Prince Philip of his plan to beat world starvation. He would melt the Himalayan snow and ice to form a huge reservoir which would be used to green the African deserts. One official at the meeting said: 'The colour of his [the prince's] face changed and he became upset. He kept repeating "hopeless, hopeless."' Saito made clear he was looking far into the future, perhaps two hundred or three hundred years. The prince replied the human species might not even last another fifty years.

The population crisis, he said, had been brought about by human genius: 'There is no getting away from the fact that our planet is facing an ecological crisis, but it has not been created by human thoughtlessness. It was not brought about by the poor, the disadvantaged and the uneducated. The very opposite: it was brought about by human scientific and technological genius. It is the creation of the most highly educated and trained people the world has ever seen.... There can be no doubt at all about the facts. The human population explosion, sustained by human science and technology, is causing almost insoluble problems for future generations. It is responsible for the degradation of the environment through the pollution of the air and the water; it is consuming essential as well as non-essential resources at a rate that cannot be sustained and, above all, it is condemning thousands of our fellow organisms to extinction.' However, the rate of population growth has been declining since the 1960s.

After forty-five years of being pilloried by the press for speaking out of turn, Prince Philip said in 2006: 'I don't have opinions about things I know nothing about.' Nevertheless in 2011 he ventured that wind farms were 'absolutely useless.' He told Esbjorn Wilmar, the owner of a company making turbines, that they would never work and they were an 'absolute disgrace.' When Wilmar argued that they were one of the most cost-effective forms of renewable energy, the prince responded: 'You don't believe in fairy tales, do you?' Wilmar then suggested that turbines should be erected on royal property. 'You stay away from my estate,' said the prince.

Plainly Philip had grasped the whole thing. Ten years earlier, he had told the Royal of Society of Arts that he had his doubts about the efficiency of wind farms, saying: 'But will they ever produce enough electricity to make the turbines go round?' Then four years later, when talking about climate change, he said: 'When they put up a whole farm of windmills off the north-east coast of Norfolk, which is on the main migratory route to Scandinavia, are we going to get sliced up ducks coming across?'

At the Chelsea Flower Show in 2008, Prince Philip was admiring the gold-medal-winning garden laid on by Australian celebrity gardener Jamie Durie. 'I do like your tree fern,' said the prince. 'Actually it's not a tree fern,' said Durie, politely correcting him. 'It's a member of the cycad family. It's a *Macrozamia moorei*.' 'I didn't want a bloody lecture,' said the Prince, stomping off.

Prince Philip rankled Prince Charles again in 2000, by opposing his stance on organic food. 'Do not let us forget we have been genetically modifying animals and plants ever since people started selective breeding,' said Philip. 'People are worried about genetically modified organisms getting into the environment. What people forget is that the introduction of exotic species – like, for instance, the grey squirrel – is going to or has done far more

121

damage than a genetically modified potato.' 'I hope he and the Prince of Wales will still be talking after this,' said Harry Hadaway of the Soil Association.

At the opening of Fasnakyle Power Station in the Scottish Highlands, Prince Philip said: 'To suggest that the power station alone destroys the beauty of Glen Affric is being as fastidious as the fairy-tale princess who could feel a pea under fifteen mattresses.'

Politics and Officialdom

At a Buckingham Palace for rank-and-file MPs, Denis MacShane, member for Rotherham, said to the Queen: 'Thank you for having me, Ma'am.' Prince Philip asked her: 'What did he say?' The Queen replied: 'He said, "Thank you for having us."' Prince Philip then said: 'Ah, Harrogate. Nice place,' leaving everyone puzzled. This was in 2001 and it was feared that the eighty-year-old prince was going deaf.

On the other hand, Prince Philip had little time for most MPs. In Ghana he was told that they had just two hundred MPs. 'That's about the right number. We have 650 and most of them are a complete bloody waste of time.'

He has little more time for government ministers, saying that you needed to buy a 'gobbledegook dictionary' to understand what they were saying and add 'an arbitrary ten years' to the promises they make. And he had a solution. He told the long-standing Paraguayan dictator General Alfredo Stroessner, who ruled the country with an iron grip from 1954 to 1989: 'It's a pleasure to be in a country that isn't ruled by its people.'

Prince Philip can give as good as he gets when it comes to MPs. At a reception for backbenchers at Buckingham Palace in 2002, the prince asked the member for Gloucester Parmjit Dhanda what he had done before he entered parliament. On hearing that he had been a student and trade union official, the prince said: 'You didn't do anything then.

Formerly a national negotiator for the information-technology union Connect, Mr. Dhanda turned to turn the question back on him, asking: 'What did you do before you were Duke of Edinburgh?' The prince replied that he had been an officer in the Royal Navy and served during the Second World War. According to another Labour MP, the prince then flicked a V-sign at Dhanda. 'It was unmistakable... bloody funny,' said the MP. 'I didn't know he had it in him.'

Attempting to laugh the whole thing off, Dhanda said the prince playfully raised one finger, not two. 'He didn't stick up two fingers,' Dhanda insisted. 'He pointed up one and said 'there you go', patting me on the shoulder before he went. He had a big smile on his face and it was very much in a sense of fun.' A palace spokeswoman said: 'The Duke of Edinburgh would certainly have no intention of making a gesture of that nature in Buckingham

Palace or anywhere else to a member of the public, let alone an MP.' And she suggested there was 'obviously not a lot going on' in the House of Commons if MPs were talking about whether the prince raised one or two fingers.

Politicians generally are giving no quarter. In *Men, Machines and Sacred Cows* he said: 'I have no sympathy with people who claim to know what is good for others.'

The prince is just as forthright with middle-class mandarins. In 1970, he told Sir Rennie Maudsley, Keeper of the Privy Purse: 'You're just a silly little Whitehall twit: you don't trust me and I don't trust you.'

In 2004, Prince Philip found himself on a barge with Tony Blair demon spin-doctor Alastair Campbell, who asked him: 'Could you drive one of these?' Philip turned a withering eye on him and barked: 'I was a bloody naval commander!'

At a reception for the 2014 Diamond Jubilee, then-Health Secretary Jeremy Hunt, who had been Culture Secretary overseeing the 2012 London Olympics, decided to tell the Queen a joke about the opening ceremony. He said: 'I read about a Japanese tourist who said afterwards how wonderful our Queen must be to take part in that, as they would never get their emperor to jump out of the plane.' The Queen grimaced, shrugged her shoulders and moved on. Next on the scene was Prince Philip. 'Who are you?' he asked Hunt. The unfortunate minister explained that he was now Health Secretary, but had been Culture Secretary at the time of the Olympics. 'They do move you people on a lot,' Prince Philip said, and moved on to the next guest.

In 1963, Prince Philip said: 'All money nowadays seems to be produced with a natural homing instinct for the Treasury.' It was true. The top rate of income tax hovered around 95 per cent in the 1960s. In 1966, The Beatles sang in the song Taxman: 'Let me tell you how it will be. There's one for you, nineteen for me.' Things had improved by 1978, but the prince still rued that crime was the only way to beat the taxman. However, the royal family did not pay income tax, capital gains tax, or inheritance tax until the Queen volunteered to do so in 1992.

At the opening of the new City Hall in 2002, Prince Philip told the members of the London Assembly who were debating the introduction of the congestion charge: 'Of course, the problem with London is the tourists. They cause the congestion. They block the streets. If we could just stop the tourism, we could stop the congestion.' Tourism brings in about an eight of the capital's GDP and its success is often attributed to the presence of the royal family.

The chairwoman of the Assembly's tourism committee, Jeanette Arnold, was quick to find fault. 'He seemed to be taking a rather rarefied view of London,' she said. 'It is clearly the sort of view only held by those who travel around in limousines.' But the prince would not be shaken on the point. On a state visit to Slovenia in 2008, he told Dr. Maja Uran, the professor of tourism at the University of Primorska: 'Tourism is just national prostitution. We do not need any more tourists. Tourists ruin cities.'

Prince Philip said of Tony Blair: 'He promises education, education, education but never delivers... Bring back Mrs. T, that's what I say. There's no one quite like Mrs. T.' After being informed of Tony Blair's re-election in 2005, he said: 'Well bugger me with a ragman's trumpet.' A lot of people felt that way, but would not have expressed it so colourfully.

At a Buckingham Palace reception in 2004, Prince Philip told Euro MP Michael Cashman that the European Union was 'all balls.' 'We should be like the Icelandic people and patrol our waters with gunboats,' Philip continued. When Cashman turned away, the prince grabbed him by the arm and hissed:

'I'm not finished with you yet.' Cashman promised to write a pamphlet about fisheries policy and sent it to him.

Asked by a teenager if he was ever nervous about meeting so many heads of state, he said: 'Well, it's surprising how you grow out of it.' Well, yes. But not so surprising if you are married to one.

Theology and Religion

Prince Philip has impeccable credentials when it comes to religion. Archbishop of York John Sentamu remarked: 'Not everyone is aware that His Royal Highness has a keen interest in theological questions. Bishops who are invited to stay and preach at Sandringham face a barrage of serious theological questions over lunch, and there is nowhere to hide. He listens appreciatively but never uncritically. In my case, the sermon was based on Jesus turning water into wine at Cana of Galilee. The duke suggested many possible explanations for the miracle, including a Uri Geller-type explanation, and he produced a spoon which Uri Geller had bent for him. To my rescue came that still small voice of calm from Her Majesty the Queen, saying: 'Philip and his theories…''' The Queen, as head of the Church of England, had the last word.

Sentamu was lucky he was not subjected to more than questioning. At a dinner party in Sandringham in 2003, Prince Philip made a mitre out of a paper napkin and made the Archbishop of Canterbury Rowan Williams wear it.

Baptised into the Greek orthodox church, Prince Philip was required to convert to Anglicanism before his marriage. 'I take an interest in comparative religion,' he said. 'But if I talk about it I'm labelled a religious crank.'

Archbishop Sentamu recalled when the Bishop of Norwich paid a pastoral visit to Sandringham, the prince asked him: 'Are you happy clappy?' 'No, I'm smells and bells,' the bishop replied. After that, they got on fine, Sentamu said.

When the Royal Yacht *Britannia* arrived at the Pier Head, Liverpool, in 1977, Prince Philip was standing alongside the Bishop of Liverpool David Sheppard when the band on the quayside struck up 'The Lord is my Shepherd.' The Prince whispered to the bishop out of the side of his mouth: 'They're playing your tune.' This was entirely unrelated to what occurred when the royal couple returned to Liverpool in 2004. At a reception to mark the centenary of Liverpool Cathedral, Prince Phillip helped himself to a couple of extra cans of brown ale, tucking them into his inside jacket pocket 'for the onward journey.'

Sometimes it seems he had little time for the clergy, telling the *New York Times* in 1984: 'Almost without exception they preach peace, good will and the brotherhood of man, and yet many of them have been used by the unscrupulous to cause more human conflict and misery than any other system, save perhaps Communism.'

Discussing the 1859 volume *Self-Help* by Samel Smiles with Lord Harris of High Cross, founder of the right-wing think-tank, the Institute for Economic Affairs, the prince said: 'I think you should arrange for every bishop in the country to have a copy. They all seem to confuse self-help and individual responsibility with selfishness.'

Prince Philip famously said of long sermons: 'The mind cannot absorb what the backside cannot endure.'

In 1957, he addressed the annual dinner of the Royal Army Chaplains. Thinking back to his own time in the services, he said: 'The tables are turned with a vengeance this evening, I cannot think how many hours I have spent at your mercy... I have got two alternatives this evening. One is to take the Old Testament doctrine of an eye for an eye, but this you can readily see has many disadvantages, including a lot of hard work for me. Or, on the other hand, I can take the New Testament doctrine and offer you the other cheek. I cannot help thinking that that would cause even more confusion. You would all have to get up and deliver a sermon at once, or one after another which would be even worse.'

Professional Bodies

At the 450th anniversary banquet of the Royal College of Surgeons in Edinburgh in June 1955, the president presented the prince with a silver replica of the cup formerly used by doctors to bleed their patients. 'And now, sir, may it please your royal highness to accept this bleeding cup?' Philip could not resist it. 'I can only say – it's bloody kind of you,' he said with a broad smile.

Becoming president of the National Playing Fields Association in 1947, Prince Philip quickly mastered the subject. Opening a playing field in Devon, he outlined the general principles. 'There is no need to have a Rolls-Royce scheme. You want a reasonably flat piece of ground with sufficient grass on it and some posts, and if you can get these you're halfway home. Put on the fancy waistcoats later.' Then addressing the opening of the National Playing Field Association exhibition in 1954, he said: 'You planners and designers may believe that you've designed the perfect layout for the perfect playing field as seen through adult eyes. But I can assure you that it may prove deadly dull to a child of four.'

As president of the Library Association, Prince Philip admitted that he did not pass muster. At their meeting in Edinburgh in 1953, he told members: 'In 1951, I was a very bad president of the Library Association. I was very bad because I spent most of that year at sea... in more ways than one.'

In June 1954, Prince Philip was made Master of the Honourable Company of Master Mariners, though he was, admittedly, unqualified for the position. 'I am feeling slightly embarrassed because I realise that the qualification of membership is, of course, a Master's Certificate, and up to a short time ago I felt I was going to be in a very undistinguished position of being the only one here without a Master's Certificate. Luckily the Minister of Transport and Civil Aviation saved me from further embarrassment by making good the deficiency, so thank you very much indeed. You are quite safe; I do not think there will be any chance of my using it.' It helps to have friends in high places.

At the annual dinner of the National Farmers' Union in February 1956, he said: 'I am now in a bit of a quandary as I am supposed to propose a toast to agriculture, and I know less about the subject than anybody else here. About four years ago I knew nothing about it at all. I could have told you that *Globirgarina ooze* is a type of seaweed, but if you asked me about proctor I could only have told you that it is a form of university police or that the king kept on about somewhere… It has been my experience that if anything goes wrong in agriculture, the farmer invariably blames the weather or the government, or both. Now, I hold no brief for the weather and no one can accuse me of having anything to do with government policy, but I think this attitude is rather unfair.'

As president of the Automobile Association, he told the annual general meeting in 1958: 'I've been made to sit in this room next door all the morning, listening to the most enormous amount of bunkum – except for the chairman of course – and at last it's my turn to add my quota of bunkum.'

In 1957, he was having lunch with the Canadian Chamber of Commerce in Great Britain when the Canadian Trade Mission were in town. 'I ought to say right away – just to get the record straight – that I accepted an invitation some month ago to lunch with the Canadian Chamber of Commerce, long before the Trade Mission was ever appointed,' he said. 'I only say that because it's not often that one can eat two lunches for the price of one.'

Speaking at the English-Speaking Union World Branches Conference in Ottawa in October 1958, he said: 'We are only just at the beginning of the vast and important contributions which the English-Speak Union can make to the world. May I hasten to add that this does not include teaching people to speak English.'

He went on to tell the English-Speaking Union that he and the Queen had attended a banquet given by the English-Speaking Union of the United States in New York the previous year. 'Next month, on 26 November, I hope to preside at a dinner in the Guildhall in London in honour of Vice-President Nixon. That, I think, puts the Commonwealth one up.' Banging the drum for the Commonwealth, he went on to say that English was 'a commonly understood language which can do so much to encourage the cohesion of that wide community who are fortunate enough to be in the Commonwealth, and those less fortunate people who are not members. Applications for membership will receive sympathetic consideration.' When Richard Nixon went on to become president of the United States in 1969, he did not apply to join.

Opening the English-Speaking Union's Symposium in London in 1960, Prince Philip said: 'The *Oxford Pocket Dictionary* gives two definitions of a symposium – 'an ancient Greek drinking party; philosophical or other friendly discussion, set of articles on one subject from various writers and points of view.' I shall assume that this symposium is intended to follow the line of the second of these definitions.' Again he drew attention to trans-Atlantic dimension of the Union. 'You will notice that heading the list of speakers is the Hon. Arthur Dean, chairman of the English-Speaking Union of the United States, and, for reasons I won't go into here, the United States is not a member of the Commonwealth. She might have been, but that is another story.'

Addressing the Canadian Medical Association in Toronto in June 1959, he said: 'I cannot help feeling that I am in a very quaint situation. Here I am, a layman, at their invitation as joint president of the Canadian and British Medical Associations, the professional holy of holies of medical men. In recent months I have frequently speculated on the reasons for this invitation without much success; but, for my part, I accepted the invitation as a great honour and privilege and as a gracious gesture on the part of the medical profession to their victims. However, I also accepted for two reasons. In the first place it would enable me to say something nice to the medical profession as a whole, on behalf of the thousands of millions of past and present patients who owe so much to the tireless and selfless work of doctors and nurses. Secondly, it seemed a perfectly marvellous opportunity to do a little preaching to the preachers. For once, a patient, although not currently suffering from anything more serious that nervous prostration, has got the medical profession or a sizable part of it in Canada and the United Kingdom at his mercy.' Later he quoted from a CMA report: 'The definition of physical fitness are presently understood and often enunciated by persons who do not base their statements on scientific observations.' He added: 'That last sentence must have been specially put in for my benefit.'

Speaking the British Medical Association four months later, he said: 'I can report that the meeting and my installation as president of the Canadian Medical Association in Toronto was a great occasion and, despite the things I said in my address there, I'm glad to say that no one threw anything at me. May I add that I expect the same considerate treatment here. For a layman and an occasional patient to find himself in this exalted position is pleasant enough but there is a distinct feeling that one must tread with caution. I am sufficiently ambitious to wish that I could do something, however small, to advance your interests, but I'm also sufficiently a realist to know that the BMA will go on performing its functions more or less successfully without any interference from me.'

A president of both the British and Canadian Medical Associations, Prince Philip refers to himself as 'Chief Medicine Man.'

Asked to present the toast 'The Craft of Surgery' at

the Royal College of Surgeons in Edinburgh he decided to pull rank. 'As patron to the college, I offer myself a hearty welcome,' he said. 'In the same breath, perhaps, I ought to give the undertaking not to attempt to practise the craft of surgery. I understand that James IV sometimes used to have a go at members of his household. Mine are quite safe. I value their assistance and friendship too highly to take that sort of liberty with them. I am gratified to become an apprentice because, though you may not believe, I can read and write. However, I take it that I am also absolved from replying that I am an Honorary Fellow of the Royal College of Surgeons of Edinburgh if anyone should ask if there is a doctor in the house.'

A joke was then in order. 'Some of you will no doubt know the story about the glamorous film star who bruised her leg on a liner,' he said. 'The purser looked through the passenger list and hurried to get help from the first doctor on the list. But the man insisted that he was a LLD [Doctor of Laws]. 'Never mind,' said the purser, 'she won't know the difference.' When the LLD got to the girl's cabin, he found he had been beaten to it by a DD [Doctor of Divinity]. The only reason the DD got there first was obviously because there was no Hon FRCSE [Honorary Fellow of the Royal College of Surgeons of Edinburgh] in that ship.'

Again he foreswore practising, again stressing his ignorance of medical matters. He had been fortunate. 'If I know nothing of the business end of surgery, so to speak, I am almost ignorant of the receiving end,' he said. 'In fact I had only been under the knife, which is an unattractive expression, twice to my certain knowledge.'

Later that same year Prince Philip was addressing the Ghana Medical Association and thanked its president for welcoming him that evening: 'Your recital of my rather more important-sounding positions might lead people to suppose that I had some sort of qualifications. Nothing could be farther from the case and my connection with medicine will always be that of an occasional but interested patient. Luckily one only needs qualifications to practise medicine, no one has ever suggested that one needs qualifications to talk about it.'

Proposing the toast 'The Common Health' at a BMA dinner in 1959, he again drew attention to the fact that he was hardly qualified to address them on the subject of medicine or health as he was not 'a hypochondriac or doctor.' He said he was rather surprised by the choice of the toast, because proposing health to doctors was like proposing a toast to pedestrians at the Society of Motor Manufacturers and Traders, or a toast to teetotallers at the Licensed Victuallers'. 'I could have understood a toast to patients,' he said. 'Or perhaps even to nurses and hospital staff – or even, at a pinch, and if you're feeling very Christian, to the Ministry of Health. But as a matter of fact, the choice of this toast this evening quite suits me, because 'Common Health' describes, I think, quite well the sort of no-man's-land between positive good health and active bad health. I couldn't help thinking of it as rather a mixture been good health, common wealth and a common cold.'

Following the toastmaster's announcement at the golden jubilee dinner of the Royal Society of Tropical Medicine and Hygiene in 1957, Prince Philip said that he felt the introduction could have stressed his credentials. 'Perhaps the toastmaster ought to have added, 'Fellow of the Royal College of Surgeons, Fellow of the Royal Society and several other organisations," he said. 'But I would like to warn you that this does not mean I necessarily know what I am talking about this evening.' However he proclaimed himself a 'satisfied customer' because of the travelling he had done. 'I don't know of the dangers or the names of the diseases I might have contracted,' he said. 'But I have in recent years visited a good many laboratories where they have been tinkering about with these things and, having seen the sort of things they are working at, I am even more grateful that I did not get them.'

In 1958, he was given honorary membership of the British Dental Association. 'There is one great disappointment though,' he said, 'and that is that you have now told me I am not allowed to practise.'

At a luncheon to celebrate the tenth anniversary of the British Association of Industrial Editors in 1959, Prince Philip again noted that they may have picked the wrong speaker. 'At first sight, it would appear that I have very little qualification to be here, or even to speak about the subject of industrial editors and house journals, or to propose this toast at all,' he said. 'Well, it just shows how wrong everybody can be, because it just so happened that I belong to an organisation that has probably got the oldest house journal going. In fact, it must be one of the first. It's called rather *The Court Circular*. I regret to say that the editor is very part-time and I am pretty sure that he does not belong to this association.'

Visiting Canada to discuss the arrangements for the second Commonwealth Conference on the Human Problems of Industrial Communities which was going to be held there in 1962, he told journalists: 'Now I cannot think of any more unsuitable subject for an after-dinner speech, even if everyone present were madly interested in it. But my orders were to tell you about this conference, so whether you like it or not you're going to hear about it. If anyone feels like throwing tomatoes, please throw them at the chap who suggested this subject.'

Addressing the annual dinner of the Chartered Insurance Institute in 1953, he again stressed his inadequacy to the task. 'I cannot help feeling somewhat surprised that you have asked me to propose this toast. As far as I know my life has never been insured, and I doubt very much whether any of my personal goods and chattels are worth insuring either. I know *Bluebottle*, *Cowslip* and *Kiwi* are insured, but you can put that down perhaps to my knowledge of marine risks, especially if I happen to be sailing them. I might, on the other hand, be interested in other forms of insurance, for instance, my Lord Mayor, excessive hospitality...'

The number of roles Prince Philip takes on can cause confusion. In May 1962, the Lord's Taverners were holding a charity luncheon at Fishmongers' Hall. As Prime Warden of the Worshipful Company of Fishmongers, it was his duty to rise and welcome the Taverners. He sat down, but then had to get up again. As patron and Twelfth Man of the Taverners, it fell to him to thank the Prime Warden, himself, for having them there. His next task as patron of the Taverners was to present the annual cheque raised by the Lord's Taverners to himself as president of the National Playing Fields Association. Then, as president of the National Playing Fields Association, he had to thank himself as the patron of the Lord's Taverners.

At the annual dinner of the Magistrates of the Metropolitan Juvenile Courts, he said: 'How sorry I am that the Chief Magistrate is not here with us this evening. I gather he is getting on well and there's nothing really very much the matter with him, and if it is any consolation to him I imagine that it is owing to his age that he escaped being run in for doing wilful damage to a lamp-post.' Prince Philip also said that he had recently discovered he was a justice of the peace.

In March 1960, Prince Philip was installed as Lord High Steward of Plymouth. In his acceptance speech to the Lord Mayor he said: 'On and off for four hundred years, Plymouth has had Lord High Stewards, and in all that time, no one seems to have settled in any great detail the duties of the Lord High Steward. One is left with the impression that the position has no duties. This, sire, suits me admirably, and I can only hope that no one tries to think of any – at least while I hold this position… I accept this position and this rod of office, which I have been instructed to return to you, sir, at once, for safe keeping.'

At the 150th anniversary dinner of the Royal Caledonian Schools at the Dorchester Hotel in London, Prince Philip noticed that the toastmaster had not, as usual, announced that, once the dinner was over, diners could smoke. 'We had some little discussion about this and I came to the conclusion that now parliament has seen fit to prevent the advertising of smoking it would be quite improper for anyone on such an occasion to do anything so improper as to say smoking might take place... I notice, however, it has not been the least discouraging.' Philip himself gave up smoking before he got married.

The Youth of Today

Despite Prince Philip's patronage of the Duke of Edinburgh Award Scheme, young people also come in for some stick. In 2006, marking its fiftieth anniversary, he was asked where the scheme was still relevant. He replied: 'Young people are the same as they always were. They are just as ignorant.' His son Prince Edward had just been given a gold Duke of Edinburgh's Award. 'But for that he would have been a dropout,' said Philip. Edward had dropped out of the Royal Marines and failed in his career in the theatre and TV. Nevertheless, Prince Philip's grandson Prince William had just passed a degree in geography. Prince Philip marked the occasion by saying: 'We get a small government grant, and I sometimes wonder, why bother?'

On another occasion, Prince Philip said: 'Any country gets the young people it deserves.' One commentator asked whether a country got the old people it deserved too.

At a Bangladeshi youth club in London's Marylebone in 2002, the Duke of Edinburgh asked youngsters:

'So who's on drugs here?' Arbitrarily spotting fourteen-year-old Shahin Ullah, the duke said: 'He look as if he's on drugs.' The teenager adamantly denied it.

Prince Philip made a similar accusation when visiting Oxford University in 2005. Spotting a traditional Egyptian 'Shisha' pipe in the room of Faizal Patel, he asked the student if he was involved in 'that sort of activity.' Then he asked the College Master: 'You let the students do this?' 'I think he thought it was a bong,' the student said later.

Talking on the radio about drug-taking, violent crime, and disrespect in 2000, Prince Philip said: 'I think there are some things which are rather disappointing. This general rather bitter, sour attitude that so many people have toward life at the moment. This aggression, boorishness and rudery... you do owe a certain amount of politeness to each other.' Fortunately, these words passed without comment.

In 2008, Prince Philip was handing a Duke of Edinburgh Award to a youngster who said he had done conservation work in Belize, 'where the SAS train, in the jungle,' the recipient said. 'Ah, Belize,' said the prince. 'A bit like Sussex.'

When the Blairs took their young son Leo to Balmoral he had been trained to recite the first verse of the National Anthem to ingratiate himself with the Queen. Knowing of Cherie's republican tendencies, Prince Philip immediately taught the boy the second verse, which goes:

> O Lord our God arise,
> Scatter her enemies,
> And make them fall:
> Confound their politics,
> Frustrate their knavish tricks,
> On Thee our hopes we fix:
> God save us all.

Handing out prizes to cadets on board the *HMS Devonshire* in 1953, Prince Philip said: 'I would like to congratulate heartily all the prize-winners and at the same time offer my sympathy to all those who were unsuccessful, an experience with which I am quite familiar.' Modesty belies the man. 'I am afraid that I am in no position to offer you any advice about your future in the Navy as I only served about half a dogwatch myself.' A dogwatch is a short watch of just two hours (instead of the usual four), from 4 to 6 pm or 6 to 8 pm, allowing the night watch to be changed every twenty-four hours. In fact, Prince Philip served in the Royal Navy from January 1940 to February 1952, only retiring when the Queen acceded to the throne. He could not have stayed on, he conceded. 'Given the way of the British press, I wouldn't have gone far in the Navy,' he said. 'Every promotion would have been seen as me being treated as a special case.' As it was, on his ninetieth birthday, the Queen made him Lord High Admiral.

The Duke of Edinburgh also ticked off a boy he found walking across the estate at Balmoral. 'You can't just wander about anywhere, you know,' he said. 'What do you think you are doing?' 'I am doing my Duke of Edinburgh's Award,' the boy replied. For once, the duke was lost for words.

Visiting the University of Salford in 2012, Prince Philip was introduced to two students, one from Liverpool, the other from Manchester, and asked, not unreasonably: 'Do you fight?' Next he came across a student with a strong Sheffield accent. 'Do you understand each other?' he asked.

Swedish rabbi Ronnie Cahana forked £32 to take his family around Windsor Castle – money that would go towards the restoration of the castle after the 1992 fire. It was to be the highlight of their visit to England and it was daughter Kitra's sixth birthday. Prince Philip had been out driving around Windsor Great Park on his carriage and stopped for the gate to be opened. 'We are royal fans and recognised him,' said Ronnie. 'My daughter loves the Queen and wondered if the duke would say Happy Birthday.' So Ronnie and six-year-old Kitra approached. 'Good morning sir, my little girl is six,' said Ronnie. 'So what?' said the prince, geeing up his horses and trotting into the stable yard, leaving the youngster in tears. 'She was very upset and crying,' said Ronnie. 'We calmed her down by saying all the other Royals were nice and he was the only nasty one.' 'Prince Philip is always extremely good with children,' said a spokesman for Buckingham Palace.

At a preview of his documentary *Around the World in Forty Minutes* it was thought that some footage of whaling was too gory for children. But Prince Philip was adamant it would be fine. 'If my children are any guide,' he said, 'there is nothing they like better than a little blood.'

Questioned by teenagers on the BBC in 1965, Prince Philip said that he missed 'just being able to walk into a cinema or go out to a night club, or go to the pub.' He could not enjoy those things because, everywhere he went, he was recognised. Then sixteen-year-old Christopher Hall asked him if there were any other countries he would like to visit. He said Russia, China and Japan. 'How do you think you'd be received in places like those?' asked Christopher. 'Oh, I think they would be reasonably polite,' the prince replied. 'Do you think they would line the streets, for instance?' Christopher persisted. 'I wouldn't say that was essential,' said Philip.

Public Speaking

In 1960, Prince Philip published *Prince Philip Speaks: Selected Speeches by His Royal Highness the Prince Philip, Duke of Edinburgh, K.G. 1956-1959.* In the introduction, he wrote: 'Some people have what I can only describe as a positive genius for saying absolutely nothing in the most charming language. Neither my English nor my imagination are good enough for that, so I try to say something which I hope might be interesting or at least constructive. To do this and at the same time to avoid giving offence can sometimes be a ticklish business. I have come to the conclusion that when in doubt it is better to play safe – people would rather be bored that offended.'

In a speech made in 1956, he had outlined his technique: 'It is my invariable custom to say something flattering to begin with so that I shall be excused if by any chance I put my foot in it later on.' Full marks for honesty.

There were other pitfalls to public speaking: 'All sorts of unexpected things can happen in speech-making. Microphones are getting more reliable but they can still play fancy tricks. Turning a page in a high wind wearing gloves and holding a sword can also be quite exciting.'

And there is always the possibility that he may something inadvertently funny: 'Gratifying but sometimes unnerving is when an audience sees a joke or something amusing in a bit that was not originally intended to be funny. This happens rather more often that I care to admit.' Naturally, this gets reported in the press. 'When, as happens from time to time, something I have said appears in 'Sayings of the Week' or similar columns, I am generally left wondering whether it was put in at face value or whether the editor has managed to read some fearfully subtle joke into something which I fondly imagined was quite ordinary.'

The prince realised that it was his role to make people laugh. 'I don't think I have ever got up to make a speech of any kind, anywhere, ever, and not made the audience laugh at least once,' he said. 'You arrive somewhere and you go down that receiving line. I get two or three of them to laugh. Always.'

Addressing the Royal Aeronautical Society in 1954, he set a benchmark, being his speech: 'If a little learning is a dangerous thing then you are in for a very dangerous address... From this you will gather that any views I express this evening must be treated with caution if nothing else.'

At a charity dinner in 1955, Prince Philip said: 'I imagine that the excellence of the dinner is designed to prevent any guests feeling that their presence here is in any way a charitable action. I take it rather more of them are demanded. You will be pleased to hear that my charitable action this evening will be a short speech, but those who cannot make speeches will have to think of something else to do.'

He had no time to sit through long speeches. At the opening of a City and Guilds of London Institute he told the foreman: 'Get weaving, I've done my bit!'

When given Freedom of the Mercers' Company in 1953, he praised the educational and charity work undertaken by the City guilds: 'It will be a very sad day if they forget their responsibility to the present and only think of their glorious past. If I may say so, you would be like baboons – all behind and no forehead.'

Prince Philip claimed to have given the best speech of his life at the opening of the Melbourne Olympic Games in 1956 – 'It consisted of exactly twelve words.'

Prince Philip noted his own shortcomings when it came to making speeches. He told an audience at

Edinburgh University in November 1953: 'This speech-making business is rather dreadful. Here I am, on my feet again, and you have all heard enough of me. I am inclined to think the only solution is to employ a professional private orator who will get up and make the proper remarks, and will then sit down again. Then there is another advantage. I can fire him if he is not funny enough and tell him to sit down if he goes on too long. Incidentally, he can write out the speeches beforehand and save all these chaps a lot of trouble.'

Addressing overseas students on the art of public speaking, Prince Philip said: 'It makes the job of the speakers so much easier if the audience is somewhat 'mellowed.' Conversely, it makes the speeches so much more tolerable – or, of course, if you have gone beyond a certain point, it makes them irrelevant, or sometimes even inaudible.' His other piece of advice was to get it over with before the last speaker is rendered completely invisible by accumulated cigar smoke.

He also pointed out the vital role of the toastmaster, especially if you are sitting next to the chairman: 'It's bad enough if he's got to worry about what he is going to say, but it's hopeless if he's also got to worry about when he's going to say it.'

North of the Border

After being educated at Gordonstoun and being made Duke of Edinburgh in 1947, Prince Philip has a special affinity for the people of Scotland. On being made Chancellor of Edinburgh University in 1953, he said: 'In education, if in nothing else, the Scotsman knows what is best for him. Indeed, only a Scotsman can really survive a Scottish education.'

In 1995, he asked Scottish driving instructor Robert Drummond in Oban: 'How do you keep the natives off the booze long enough to pass the test?'

In December 1999, after meeting three workers from a Scottish salmon farm at Holyrood Palace, the prince said: 'Oh! You're the people ruining the rivers and the environment.'

In 1992, the royal family suffered an *annus horribilis* when their Berkshire home caught fire, causing £36.5-million of damage. 'People say after a fire it's water damage that's the worst. We're still drying out Windsor Castle,' Philip said.

Prince Philip further annoyed the Scots by referring to the Firth of Forth as the Filth of Firth because of the pollution in it. In 1979, the standard for cleanliness in Britain generally came in for royal disapproval when he declared that the UK was 'one of the dirtiest countries anywhere.'

In 1960, the prince told an audience at the Waldorf-Astoria: 'Scotland is not entirely peopled by huge men in kilts with hairy legs, who drink whisky when they are not playing the bagpipes or tossing the caber.' Just mostly populated, then.

In a Radio 5 interview shortly after the Dunblane shootings in 1996, where a gunman killed one teacher and sixteen primary-school pupils, injuring fifteen more, Prince Philip was asked if guns should be banned. He said: 'If a cricketer, for instance, suddenly decided to go into a school and batter a lot of people to death with a cricket bat, which he could do very easily, I mean, are you going to ban cricket bats?' Afterwards he said to the interviewer off-air: 'That will really set the cat among the pigeons, won't it?'

In 2006, Prince Philip visited the Caledonian Club in Belgravia (though he had been an honorary member since 1948) only to shock his hosts with the quip: 'I'm just wondering what happens when Scotland goes independent?' 'The Duke of Edinburgh has obviously been reading the opinion polls,' said Alex

Salmond.

The duke was then presented with a silver tankard, engraved with the deer-stalking areas of the Balmoral estate. 'It's unusual to get something useful, 'he said with a grin.

Being given the Freedom of the City of Glasgow in 1955, Prince Philip said: 'The freedom of a city is looked up by those who give it and those who receive it as a very great honour indeed and the ceremony is full of charm and dignity.' Then in reference to the old music-hall song, he added: 'Unlike the ownership of Glasgow, which, I understand, can be obtained for a couple of drinks on a Saturday night.'

The Welsh sometimes get some teasing, too. At a walkabout in Chippenham, Wilshire, in 2001, the prince stopped to speak to old soldier Jack Spencer. When the war veteran said he had served in the Third Monmouthshire Regiment, Philip replied incredulously: 'What do you want to go to Wales for?' (Mr. Spencer responded that his grandfather was a Welshman).
Later the Duke poked fun at the Welsh again as he talked to farm stall manager Jean Pocock. Picking a leek from the stall and brandishing it, the prince asked: 'Do any Welsh people live here?'

Johnny Foreigner

The Times of London said it best: 'The Duke of Edinburgh is notorious for his 'jokes,' but he really only has one, single, transferrable joke, and it goes like this: foreigners are odd; they look peculiar, eat strange things, and may be lumped into groups according to national or racial characteristics; this is funny.'

Visiting China in 1986, he said toaBritish exchange student in Xian: 'If you stay here much longer, you'll go home with slitty eyes.' The *Daily Mirror* called him: 'The Great Wally of China'; while the *Sun* said: 'The duke gets it wong

Later in 1986, he told a meeting of the World Wildlife Fund: 'If it has four legs and it's not a chair, if it's got two wings and it flies but is not an aeroplane and if it swims and it's not a submarine, the Cantonese will eat it.'

In February 2013, when opening in £5.5-million cardiac centre at the Luton and Dunstable Hospital, Prince Philip told a Filipino nurse: 'The Philippines must be half-empty – you're all here running the NHS.' Everybody laughed. Indeed, according to the Nursing and Midwifery Council, there were 16,184 Filipino nurses in the UK.

At a Buckingham Palace reception, Prince Philip met cultural worker Sukhvinder Stubbs. 'And are you from Guyana?' said the prince. 'Er, no I'm from India,' said Stubbs. 'Hmph,' responded Philip, 'I'm sure there are Indians in Guyana. They get everywhere, don't they.'

At a Christmas party for royal staff in Buckingham Palace in 2003, Prince Philip pointed to the turban of Sikh policeman Sarinder Singh and wondered: 'How on earth do you get that under your helmet?'

In 2003, while on a state visit to Nigeria, Prince Philip attended a formal reception hosted by the then-president of Nigeria Olusegun Obasanjo. Dressed to receive his royal visitor, the president was wearing his resplendent national dress, an elaborately embroidered billowing robe known as an *agbada*. The Prince took one look at the garment and exclaimed: 'You look like you're ready for bed!'

He had been no more diplomatic during the ceremony giving Kenya its independence in 1963. Just as the Union Jack was being lowerd, hehe turned to Jomo Kenyatta, the country's new prime minister, and asked 'Are you sure you want to go through with this?' The Kenyan flag was raised as arranged, despite

Kenyatta's joking answer of 'no.'

Plainly the prince has learnt his lesson over the years. When asked in Nigeria in 2003: 'So what do you think of Africa?' He replied: 'I'll pass on that if you don't mind.'

He was little more sympathetic to African art. When shown an example from Ethiopia in 1965, he said: 'It looks like the kind of thing my daughter would bring back from school art lessons.'

BBC Formula One TV presenter and former Jordan team boss Eddie Jordan was part of the welcoming committee in Dublin when the Queen visited in 2011. Prince Philip walked up to him and said: 'Ah! You're that funny chap who does the F1.' The following year the funny chap was given an honorary OBE.

On a trip to Berlin in 2004, Prince Philip met two students who both said that they were from Ballyclare, County Antrim in Northern Ireland. 'At last we've got two Irishmen in the same room agreeing with each other,' said the prince. The Queen had just made a speech, urging the British and Germans to 'learn from history, not be obsessed by it' and 'to look beyond simplistic stereotypes.'

In 1974, two Irish nuns turned up with a party of schoolchildren making a special outing to the palace. 'I hope you are not going to blow us up with your concealed bombs,' said the prince. The Provisional IRA were active on the mainland at the time.

Greeting a farmer's wife from Northern Ireland at a charity event in 2004, Prince Philip commented: 'So you managed to get here without having your knickers blown off.' By then the IRA campaign on the mainland was over.

In La Paz in Bolivia, Prince Philip was asked why he had not brought the famous photographer Lord Snowdon, then his brother-in-law, with him. The prince replied: 'Britain is a democracy. I get what photographer I'm given.' In Valparaisco, Chile, the prince appealed to one photographer to stop following him around. 'We have one in the family already,' he said.

On a walkabout in Abu Dhabi in 2010 he asked British expats: 'Are you running away from something?' Spotting Lieutenant Colonel Ledger of the Queen's Royal Hussars, of which Prince Philip is colonel-in-chief, he asked: 'Why have you fled?' Ledger explained that he was working for the British Government in the United Arab Emirates. Prince Philip then refused to shake the hands of a string of children in the ninety-degree heat, explaining: 'I've got to get back to work.' Further along the line eleven-year-old Jack Morgan stuck his hand out and asked for a shake. Prince Philip asked: 'Why?' (but eventually relented).

In 2010, Prince Philip was showing the multinational benefactors of Cambridge University around Windsor Castle and demonstrated his sensitivity towards foreign visitors. Entering the Waterloo Chamber, built to commemorate the victory over Napoleon in 1815, he said: 'If you happen to be French, it's the music room.'

Although Prince Philip is worshipped as a god by the islanders of Tanna in Vanuatu, he is notoriously forthright when it comes to native peoples. On visiting the Tjapukai Aboriginal Cultural Park in northern Queensland, he was told that the park was run by two Aboriginal tribes, the Djabugay and the Yirrganydji. He responded: 'Djabugay, Yirrganydji, what's it all about? Do you still throw spears at each other?' The park's founder, William Brin, appeared to choke with surprised laughter. 'No, we don't do that any more,' replied Mr. Brim, whose indigenous name is Ngoo Nvi, meaning platypus. 'I don't mind; it was quite funny,' he said later. 'I'd call the question naive.' In fact, Aboriginals who maintain the traditional lifestyle do use spears to inflict tribal punishments and one of their most guarded tribal traditions is a ritual spear-throwing ceremony, which is a rite of passage. The royal couple then watched a ten-minute display of Aboriginal music and dance, the highlight of which was a fire-lighting ceremony using fire

161

sticks and dry grass. As one performer rubbed the sticks close to another man, the prince joked: 'You've set fire to him,' adding: 'This is just like being back in the Scouts!'

In 2000, on a visit to Canberra, Aborigine didgeridoo player Bob Slockee told the prince that he had learnt to play by puffing on the pipe from a vacuum cleaner. Philip said: 'I hope it wasn't turned on at the time.' Then examining Bob's instrument, he said: 'I hope you haven't got anything inside that tube?'

But Prince Philip's caustic wit was not confined to the Aboriginals. In Cairns, when a school band played 'God Save the Queen,' he said to the children: 'You were playing your instruments, weren't you? Or do you have tape recorders under your seats?' And he insisted that a piezometer, used in the cotton industry to measure the depth of water in soil, was 'a pissometer.' 'No,' said an Aussie farmer. 'I'll spell it for you.'

During the coronation tour of Australia, Prince Philip found a way to amuse himself on long car journeys. He would look out for Aussies leaning on the lampposts outside pubs and wave at them. When they tried to wave back, they would lose their grip on the lamppost and fall over drunk.

In 2011, Prince Philip was back in Australia. At the

opening ceremony of the Commonwealth Heads of Government meeting in Perth, he was watching a troupe of Aboriginals perform in native dress and said: 'You won't see that in the Outback.'

When opening an annexe to Vancouver City Hall in 1987, he said: 'I declare this thing open, whatever it is.'

Speaking on the key problems that faced Brazil, he simply said: 'Brazilians live there.' On a state visit to the country in 1968, he said: 'The man who invented the red carpet needed his head examined.'

Introduced to a military man with chest full of medals, Prince Philip asked him where he got them. 'In the war,' the general told him. 'I didn't know Brazil was in the war that long,' said the Prince. After the middle of 1942, the Brazilian navy and air force played a role in the Battle of the Atlantic and the 25,700 men of the Brazilian Expeditionary Force fought in Italy from September 1944 to May 1945, losing 948 killed in action. The general replied: 'At least, sir, I didn't get them from marrying my wife.'

On another occasion Prince Philip asked a Sri Lankan veteran who had turned out with a chest full of medals: 'Have you got any on the back too?'

Prince Philips admitted to being a bogus holder of

the Burma Star, a medal given to those who had served in the Burma campaign against the Japanese between 1941 and 1945. Though he had served in the Pacific, he had never gotten closer to Burma than Ceylon, now Sri Lanka. 'I can't say I'm sorry,' he said, 'because I'm not particularly fond of rain and I understand that campaign umbrellas were frowned upon.'

At a breakfast to mark the 200th anniversary of St. James's barbers, Truefitt & Hill, Prince Philip was approached by one reporter, who 'wondered if he might like to talk to her.' He brushed her aside with the riposte: 'Well, you can carry on wondering.' Plunging into his speech, he said: 'There's an interesting bunch of you who no doubt come here to have your hair cut, although there are a couple of obvious exceptions." Addressing some foreigners present, he said: 'You people from Iceland no doubt come here to have your beards trimmed.'

In the Solomon Islands in 1982, when he was told that the annual population growth was five percent, Prince Philip said: 'Five percent! You must be out of your minds. You'll have a massive economic crisis in twenty years' time and blame everybody else.'

In 1998 during an official visit to Papua New Guinea, Prince Philip said to a British student who had been trekking along the Kokoda jungle trail: 'You managed not to get eaten then?'

Actor and former MP Gyles Brandreth recalled an incident in 1984 where Prince Philip introduced him to a distinguished, Indian-looking gentleman wearing a bright summer suit and an overblown rose in his buttonhole. 'This is the president of Pakistan,' the prince said before wandering away. Brandreth found himself completely out of his depth. When Prince Philip came back, he asked: 'How are you two getting on?' Brandreth was still struggling to make small talk. The prince listened for a moment to what he was saying and then interrupted: 'He's the president of the Pakistan Playing Fields Association, you idiot. He is not General Zia.' General Mohammad Zia-ul-Haq had made himself president of Pakistan after a bloodless coup in 1977, though the former prime minister Zulfikar Ali Bhutto and Zia's patron was executed two years later. He declared martial law, banned political parties and trades unions, imposed strict censorship of the press and began in the Islamisation of Pakistan before dying in a plane crash in 1988.

During a reception at Buckingham Palace for the four hundred most influential British Asians in 2009, Prince Philip spotted the name badge of business chief Atul Patel and said: 'There's a lot of your family in tonight.' Indeed there are some 670,000 Patels living in the UK.

Ten years earlier, Prince Philip had caused a similar controversy when he was inspecting a factory in Scotland and spotted an outdated fuse box. 'It looks as though it was put in by an Indian,' he said. Two hours and fourteen minutes later, Buckingham Palace backtracked. 'I meant to say cowboys,' the prince said. 'I just got my cowboys and Indians mixed up.'

A man of unerring aim, Prince Philip can write off anything that does not pass muster with one word: 'Ghastly.' That was his opinion of Beijing when he accompanied the Queen on a state visit in 1986.

Refusing to stroke a koala in Australia in 1992, he said: 'Oh no, I might catch some ghastly disease.'

In New Zealand, Prince Philip declined an opportunity to try his hand at sheep shearing, saying: 'Not on your life. I might nick him, and we've had quite enough mutton on this tour already, thank you.'

When the prince visited the Hanover Trade Fair in 1997, he greeted German chancellor Helmut Kohl as '*Reichskanzler*' – a title that died with Hitler. Since 1947, the elected leader in Germany has the rather less imperious title *Bundeskanzler*, or 'Federal Chancellor.'

In 2000, he told guests at a reception marking the

opening of the new £18-million British Embassy in Berlin that it was 'a vast waste of space.' However, later, when a journalist asked: 'Your Royal Highness, could you give us your view on the building?' He said simply: 'No.'

Prince Philip is at his most direct when it comes to foreign affairs. Back in 1967, he was asked whether he would like to visit the Soviet Union. He replied: 'I would like to go to Russia very much – although the bastards murdered half my family.' (He was the great-nephew of the last Tsarina, Alix of Hesse, who was killed along with her husband and family by the Bolsheviks in Yekaterinburg in 1918. His DNA was used to identify the remains of her and her children).

In the 1950s, Prince Philip had said to one French Minister of the Interior: 'Too bad you sent your royal family to the guillotine.' But, he counselled: 'Getting angry about history is a sterile occupation.'

In 1994, the prince asked Cayman Islander William Tennent, a museum curator: 'Aren't most of you descended from pirates?' Indeed, as there appears to have been no native Amerindians on the Cayman Islands before the arrival of Europeans, most of the early inhabitants were pirates, along with refugees from the Spanish Inquisition, shipwrecked sailors and slaves. It is now the home for tax exiles, which are often the same thing.

At a Commonwealth conference, Prince Philip charmed the leaders of the tiny South Pacific island Nauru, home to a huge phosphate mine. 'So you're from Nauru, eh?' said the prince. 'Haven't they dug it all up yet?'

In 2005, when London won the bid to host the 2012 Olympic Games, the prince, then eighty-four, told Cherie Blair: 'I'm so old I won't be here.' He was, but he was no big fan. He told the *Daily Telegraph* that he detests them so much that he planned to do 'as little as possible' during the London Olympics in 2012. 'Opening and closing ceremonies ought to be banned. Absolute bloody nuisances,' he said. 'I have been to one that was absolutely appallingly awful. At the Olympics in the old days, when they were more or less amateur, the last event of the whole Games was the show jumping in the main stadium because the horses used to cut up the ground. Well, blow me down I was suddenly told, at Munich I think it was, that we couldn't have the main arena for show jumping because it had to be prepared for the 'Closing Ceremony.' So, I said: 'What is the Olympics about? The competition or the closing ceremony?' So I am truly fed up with opening and closing ceremonies. They're a pain in the neck.'

In at a Commonwealth Day party in 1999, Prince Philip asked Tory politician Lord Taylor of Warwick:

'And what exotic part of the world do you come from?' He replied: 'Birmingham.' His parents came from Jamaica.

During President Barack Obama's visit to the UK in 2009 for a meeting of the G20 leaders, he told Prince Philip: 'I had breakfast with the prime minister [then Gordon Brown]. I had meetings with the Chinese, the Russians, David Cameron.' The prince replied: 'Can you tell the difference between them?' Observers said they believed he was referring to the meetings, not the people.

After meeting exchange students who were coming to Britain during a visit to Brunei in 1998, he said: 'I don't know how they're going to integrate in places like Glasgow and Sheffield. I had to commiserate with them.'

In 1956, at a dinner to mark the three-hundredth anniversary of the return of Jews to Britain, the prince said: 'I am in a bit of quandary this evening. The three hundredth anniversary of the resettlement of the Jews in the British Isles seems as good an excuse as any to have a party and an excellent dinner. I think it is also most appropriate that I should propose this toast to the Anglo-Jewish community. But here's the snag: do I congratulate the ancestors of this community on having the good sense to come here in the first place? Or do I congratulate the community on having stuck it here for three hundred years?'

Philip is sensitive about his Greek heritage. For the Queen's golden jubilee, he rejected the design of a ceremonial carved pear-wood chair made for him because it incorporated olives. They were, he said, 'too foreign' and 'not British enough'. At the last minute, the olives were replaced with carved bay leaves. However, bay also comes from the Mediterranean and bay leaves were used to crown victorious athletes in ancient Greece.

While competing in the Fastnet Race, crewmen of a boat approaching the prince's vessel yelled 'water' – a yachtsman's term for moving out of the way – followed by 'Stavros,' a reference to his Greek origins. The prince shouted back: 'It's not Stavros and it's my wife's f***ing water and I'll do what I f***ing please in it.' Princess Diana always referred to Philip as Stavros and to her in-laws in general as 'the Germans.'

t a prize-giving ceremony for the Duke of Edinburgh Awards in 2010, a girl told him that she had been to Romania to help in an orphanage. He replied: 'Ah good, there's so many of those orphanages over there you feel they breed them just to put in orphanages.' Prince Charles is a patron of FARA, a charity helping Romanian orphans.

During a Royal visit to a Murugan Hindu temple in north London in 2002, Prince Philip asked the four priests which part of Sri Lanka they were from. One said: 'We are from the north and east of the island. We are Tamils.' The prince than asked: 'Are you Tigers?' The Tamil Tigers were a terrorist group in Sri Lanka, defeated in 2009. No one said anything for a few minutes and then the priest explained: 'No, we are priests. We are not associated with violence.' Later he insisted that no offence had been taken at what the prince said. 'He does say interesting things, doesn't he? It must be his sense of humour we keep reading about so much. We were not offended. We blessed him with a long life and health and peace.'

After a visit to a Hindu temple in Gujarat, Prince Philip asked a journalist: 'Have you seen the one in Neasden? It's exactly the same, only bigger.'

The prince always had problems with the subcontinent. At a conference in Washington in 1956, he asked an Asian gentleman: 'Are you Indian or Pakistani? I can never tell the difference with you chaps.'

In 1955, Dr. Salvador Allende, then a member of the Chilean senate, was attending a state banquet at Buckingham Palace. Observing that Allende was wearing a lounge suit, Prince Philip demanded: 'Why are you dressed like that?' Allende explained: 'Because my party is poor, they advised me not to hire evening dress.' The prince countered imperiously: 'I suppose if they told you to wear a bathing costume, you would come dressed in one.' Dr. Allende went on to become president of Chile and died in a coup in 1973.

On a visit to Ghana, Prince Philip was shown a strip of brass in a churchyard that marked the Prime Meridian. 'A line in the ground, eh? Very nice,' he said. It is, of course, how the Meridian is marked in Greenwich as well.

At a Malawi Independence Celebration in July 1964, an African waiter whacked a photographer over the head with a wooden sign as he was focussing on Prince Philip, who said: 'Now, that wasn't a friendly gesture, was it?'

The prince is perhaps aware of reactions to his offensive comments to foreigners. When asked about the situation in South Africa in the 1960s during apartheid, he told a press conference: 'Almost anything I say will be taken down and used in evidence against me.'

Arriving at the airport in Delhi in 1959, he was saluted by a visiting US Navy lieutenant. 'Ah,' said Prince Philip, 'So I see you've joined the

Commonwealth.'

At a dinner of the English-Speaking Union in June 1957, Prince Philip greeted the US ambassador John Hay Whitney, saying: 'I don't know how Mr. Whitney was chosen for his present job, but his qualifications make it very easy for anyone proposing his health. His grandfather, John Hay, held this post sixty years ago. Mr. Whitney himself went to Oxford, fought with the United States Air Force in the European theatre, was taken prisoner and escaped, and breeds race-horses. I think he must have had his eye on this post for quite a long time; those qualifications cannot have been fortuitous. On top of all this, he was obviously gifted with second sight. He foresaw this dinner and this speech, so he thoughtfully took up polo as well.'

At the 150th anniversary banquet of the Canada Club, held at the Guildhall in 1960, Prince Philip was proposing a toast and said: 'What a very great pleasure and honour it is for me to be able to preside... and also to wear this very delightful badge which was given for the chairman to wear on these occasions, and I can tell you so far I've managed to keep it out of the food.'

There are, of course, perks to the prince's duties. At a farewell dinner in Accra after a state visit to Ghana in 1959, he was presented with an inkstand made of

ivory and gold. In his acceptance speech, he said:
'Only the other day I found myself sympathising with
the minister of finance about his little problem of
paying for the next five-year plan. Now that I have
accepted this present, I won't be able to look him in
the face.'

In 1962, Prince Philip was asked whether a British
businessman travelling to Latin America should wear
a bowler hat or a sombrero. 'It doesn't really matter,'
he said. 'But it would be better to send a bowler-
hatted man speaking Spanish, than a man wearing a
sombrero who could only speak English.'

More Princely Antipodean Balls

When Australian Prime Minister Robert Menzies serenaded the Queen impromptu in Queens Hall, 'I did but see her passing by, and yet I love her 'til I die', she blushed deeply, then, catching Prince Philip's eye, in a rare crack in royal decorum, the couple sniggered.

On New Zealand, the prince had a few pointed thoughts: on Maori—they are being treated like 'museum pieces and domestic pets', he wrote to an Australian politician in 1954.

In the same letter, he said, it is 'over- governed with not much room for initiative' and so 'the perfect welfare state'.

Even so, he conceded that he thought New Zealanders were 'universally charming and on the whole most considerate'.

On meeting Cate Blanchett, the Oscar-winning actress, in 2008 she told him she worked in the film industry, and he asked her with delight, 'There's a cord sticking out of the back of the machine. Might you tell me where it goes?'

At a garden party in Perth in October 2011, the prince commented on the fashion sense of Australia's richest person, mine-owner Gina Rinehart, and warned her, 'That hat could poke someone's eye out'.

In 1981, on the occasion of the Queen opening Tawa's memorial paddling pool he told one whispered in the ear of a New Zealand comedian that he liked the sound of a 'piddling pool'.

On Australia and the monarchy, the prince bluntly said, 'If the monarchy is of value, retain it. If not, get rid of it.'

The Press and Media

There is perhaps no relationship more contentious than Prince Philip and the British press. The press gets a kick out of his supposed gaffes and sass, and the prince has accepted this somewhat brutal portrayal: 'There we are. I've become a caricature. I've just got to live with it.' On reading himself in the press: 'As so often happens, I discover that it would have been better to keep my mouth shut.' Later he realized: 'I reckon I have done something right if I don't appear in the media,' and vowed to change: 'I've retreated – quite consciously – so as not to be an embarrassment.'

The prince was well aware of the disappointment he caused when he did not live up to his reputation. 'When we were in South Africa some years ago, I flew up to Kimberley and was persuaded to take some media people with me,' he explained. 'On the way back, one of them said to my policeman that it had been a waste of time as I had not put my foot in it.

Although he has complained of being 'frequently misrepresented,' the prince has learned to live with hostile media and only judges as he sees fit: 'I don't hate the press; I find a lot of it is very unpalatable.

But if that's the way they want to behave, well…' It seems he'll let it speak for itself.

To those who might be sensitive to feelings of misunderstanding, the prince gives a dose of reality: 'You cannot take quotations in newspapers seriously. It so happens that it is perfectly legal to put anything in a newspaper in quotation marks, and there is nothing you can do about it. You have no copyright on what other people say you said.'

On the other hands, he never did much to endear himself to the press. In 1950, on being shown the Barbary apes on Gibraltar, he remarked: 'Which are the press and which are the apes?'

He cannot overcome his distaste and is always on the defensive when it comes to the press. One British reporter recalled approaching Prince Philip with a positive comment, but the prince fended off the approach nonetheless with a convenient defence mechanism:
an electronic buzzer in his pocket and that sent the police running.

Prince Philip's biographer Tim Heald revealed how every day, wherever he is, the prince makes a grab for the newspapers saying: 'Let's see what I'm supposed to have done wrong
    The newspaper strike in 1955 seemed to provide a

respite from this cynical experience: 'Breakfast seemed to take no time at all.' The newspaper strike in 1955 seemed to provide a respite from this cynical experience: 'Breakfast seemed to take no time at all.'

The prince always makes sure to speak to the press with candour. In 1980, veteran *Sun* photographer Arthur Edwards was sitting in his car outside the stables at Sandringham, talking to a friend, when Prince Philip stuck his head through the window and said: 'Having a good snoop, are we?'

Sometimes, the prince gets a taste of his own medicine when the press dishes out their own sass. Once, the dirty-raincoat brigade was loitering by the gates of Sandringham when Prince Philip drove up in his Land Rover. 'You people are scum,' he bawled out of the window. The veteran royal correspondent of the *Sun* rose to the challenge: 'We may be scum, sir,' he retorted, 'but we are the *crème de la scum*.'

In 2007, Prince Philip was asked by a journalist about the bruising on his face. 'Do I look bloody ill?' he replied. He had slipped over in the bath.

At a reception at Windsor Castle to market the Queen's Golden Jubilee in 2002, Philip asked *The Independent*'s Simon Kelner, an outspoken republican: 'Who are you?' Kelner replied: 'I'm the editor-in-chief of *The Independent*.' Unimpressed, the prince said: 'What are you doing here?' Kelner replied deferentially: 'You invited me, sir.' Philip snapped back: 'Well, you didn't have to come.'

The editors of downmarket tabloids fare no better. When the editor of the *Daily Mirror* introduced himself to the prince, he said: 'God, you can't tell from the outside, can you?' But then, the editor in question was Piers Morgan.

Another victim was Martin Townsend, editor of the *Sunday Express*. 'Ah, the *Sunday Express*,' said Philip when they were introduced. 'I was very fond of Arthur Christiansen' – editor of the *Daily Express* from 1933 to 1957. 'Yes, there's been a long line of distinguished editors,' said Townsend. 'I didn't say that!' the Prince snapped, making his point clear as he walked away.

In Bangladesh in 1983, the Royal couple were greeting the guests at a cocktail party when Prince Philip spotted the arrival of the press. He turned to the Queen and said: 'Here come the bloody reptiles' – a sentiment *Private Eye* usually attributes to Denis Thatcher.

If at worst they were 'the bloody reptiles,' then at best journalists were 'the people's ambassadors,' as the prince referred to them at the Foreign Press Association anniversary dinner in 1948, where he was guest of honour. It would have been nearly a compliment, too, if he had not added dryly: 'And if I may say so, I often wish the people didn't want to know quite so much.'

When asked by the British Parliamentary Press Gallery to give his views on journalists in general in 1956, Prince Philip was uncharacteristically reticent. 'It is very tempting,' he said, 'but I think I had better wait until I get a bit older.' He was capable of a backhanded compliment though. 'Seriously,' he said, 'I think that journalism, like any other great institution in this country, is capable of both the best and the worst. In fact, I think that our journalism very accurately reflects our nature, both with the lid on and with the lid off. But personally, all I can say is that there are times when I would very much like to be a newspaper owner.'

In 1954, in a leading article, the *Daily Mirror* said that the royal family had nothing better to do than sit at home and 'twiddle their thumbs.' On a visit to the Ford Dunlop factory in Birmingham, Prince Philip hit back, saying: 'Of course, ladies and gentlemen, you know what I am doing – I am twiddling my thumbs.'

Visiting the White House in 1957, the royal couple were posing for photographs on the steps. As they turned to go, an American photographer yelled: 'Hey, just one more!' Cleary the man had overstepped protocol and Prince Philip barked back: 'What do you mean, just one more?'

At a dinner for the Newspaper Press Fund in May 1955, Prince Philip said: 'I am in a bit of a quandary this evening because I can't very well talk about charity all the time, in which case I'm left with the press and, quite frankly, I'd rather be left with a baby… On the other hand, it would be ungracious and hardly tactful to criticise any aspect of the press, particularly after such a good dinner, and it might also prejudice your charitable frame of mind. I don't know how easy it is for a journalist to work up a charitable frame of mind.' The Newspaper Press Fund was set up in 1864 to assist journalists and their dependants who had fallen on hard times – it is now known as the Journalists' Charity.

At a Press Association lunch in June 1963, he responded to an article saying he had been over-quoted and over-photographed. 'It is encouraging to know that at least I am being killed by kindness,' he said.

In March 1962, he said: 'The *Daily Express* is a bloody awful newspaper.' Few could disagree with that. But he went on to say that it was 'full of lies, scandal and imagination… a vicious newspaper'. No change there then.

At the Newspaper Society Golden Jubilee lunch in 2002, Prince Philip asked a guest which local paper he worked for. 'I'm terribly sorry sir, but I'm an impostor,' replied the journalist. 'I'm from the Peterborough column of the *Daily Telegraph*.' 'Don't worry,' said the Prince. 'It's not your fault.'

At a state banquet in Paris in 1996, Prince Philip said to President Jacques Chirac: 'If we had your laws, the British press could not have done so much damage to the royal family.' Thanks, in part, to the investigative work of the satirical newspaper *Le Canard enchaîné*, Chirac was convicted of embezzlement and other corruption charges in 2011.

He has little patience for the press to begin with, not to mention the less-than-hard-hitting questions. After a banquet in the Élysée Palace, BBC reporter Caroline Wyatt asked if the Queen was enjoying her trip to Paris, Prince Philip replied: 'Damn fool question!'

In 2004, when BBC newsreader Michael Buerk told Prince Philip he knew about the Duke of Edinburgh's Gold Awards, the prince replied: 'That's more than you know about anything else then.'

This was a little harsh as Michael Buerk had commentated at the royal wedding of Prince Edward and Sophie Rhys-Jones in 1999. However, Buerk had gone on to award Ryan Parry with the prestigious

Hugh Cudlipp medal at the British Press Awards for 'excellence in popular tabloid journalism' after the twenty-six-year-old *Daily Mirror* reporter had used a fake CV to get a job as a footman in Buckingham Palace. Ryan revealed Prince Edward's love of teddy bears, Prince Andrew's use of colourful language, Princess Anne's taste in black bananas and that the Queen and Prince Philip kept their cereals in a Tupperware box.

When ITN did a live-to-camera piece on Prince Philip's romantic gesture of taking the Queen back to Malta for their sixtieth wedding anniversary, he crept up behind the reporter and loudly yelled *'finished!'* causing her to jump before bursting into laughter.

Similar antics were had at the Seventy-fifth Royal Variety Performance in Edinburgh, when he turned to a journalist and asked 'Bloody hell, they've dragged you all the way up here, have they?'

In 1966, the matron of a hospital Prince Philip was visiting in the West Indies apologized for the pestering mosquitos. The prince seemed to sympathize: 'I know what you mean,' he said. 'You have mosquitoes. I have the press.'

At a press conference at London Airport in 1966, a TV crew that tried shoving a microphone under his nose was met with sass. 'Here comes that bloody machine again,' he said. 'Why don't you take the thing and stuff it up…' The next few words were inaudible. 'You wouldn't like it.'

Although at first he resisted participating in the documentary *The Duke at 90*, he eventually agreed, insisting: 'We're not a secret society. I don't see why people shouldn't know what's going on. Much better that they should know than speculate.' Nevertheless, the media was intrusive. 'The media is a professional intruder,' he said. 'You can't complain about it.' Although, of course, he did.

On pressing media: 'People only want to know about the splashy things, or the scandalous things. They're not really interested in anything else. What you want is a *Dynasty* production where everybody can see what we do privately.' 'The press have turned us into a soap opera,' he said on another occasion.

Press photographers were the bane of his existence. 'I go out of my way to line people up for the photographers,' he said, 'to make sure everyone in the group is in the picture, to make sure the photographers have got the shot they need… Of course, they always want one more. They're never satisfied.'

The prince's resentment for the press even comes in many languages! A French photographer was once admonished with the line '*Vous etes fou, restez chez vous*' – 'You are a fool, go home.'

The press often deliberately antagonise Prince Philip, knowing that he might snap back giving them a juicy quote and a good picture. In 1987 in Trinidad, he turned on reporters and snarled: 'You lot have ruined my life.' Journalists seized the opportunity to point out that Philip had arrived in Britain homeless and penniless and had risen to live a life of absolute privilege, with an income then of £200,000, castles and palaces to live in, sixteen weeks' holiday a year and an army of servants to cater for his every whim. Hardly a life in ruins.

Finale

At the age of seventy-eight, Prince Philip already felt the end was near. This didn't seem to worry him, though: he told a royal biographer 'It's much better to go while you're still capable, than wait till people say you're so doddery, it's time you went.'

On turning eighty, Prince Philip said: 'I'm not sure I recommend it. It's not so much the age, but trying to survive the celebrations.'

More than thirty members of the Royal Family, including seventeen of his German relations, turned out for his eightieth birthday party. The celebrations included twenty boy dancers dressed in sailor suits who performed a specially choreographed Duke's hornpipe. At the end of it, they produced flags and wished him a happy birthday in semaphore. Prince Philip was sure to credit the fact that he remained fit and well to all the toasts to his health.

In 2011, he was given an Oldie of the Year Award as 'Consort of the Year.' Unable to attend the lunch at Simpson's in The Strand to accept it, he sent a handwritten note, saying 'I much appreciate your invitation to receive an 'Oldie of the Year Award.' There is nothing like it for morale to be reminded that the years are passing – ever more quickly – and that bits are beginning to drop off the ancient frame.'

On ageing gracefully: 'You don't really want nonagenarians as heads of organisations which are trying to do something useful. There is an ageism in this country, as everywhere, and quite rightly so, because I think you go downhill – physically, mentally and everything. It's better to get out before you reach the sell-by date.'

Passing ninety years old, he admitted: 'I reckon I've done my bit, I want to enjoy myself for a bit now. With less responsibility, less rushing about, less preparation, less trying to think of something to say. On top of that your memory's going, I can't remember names. Yes, I'm just sort of winding down.'

When it was suggested that he might hope to live to be a hundred, Prince Philip assured us: 'I am not, I can tell you.' The question is, if he did, would he get a telegram from the Queen?

Biography

Prince Philip, Duke of York, is a national treasure. He is a throwback to a time when Britannia ruled the waves and when the royal families of Europe interbred: the Queen is his third cousin; they share a great-great-grandmother in Queen Victoria; his mother Princess Alice of Battenberg and sister of Lord Mountbatten was born in the Tapestry Room in Windsor Castle.

Despite his disrupted childhood and general penury, Prince Philip has led a successful and exciting life. In 1939, when King George VI and Queen Elizabeth visited the Royal Naval College, Prince Philip escorted his cousins Princess Elizabeth and Princess Margaret, and the future queen (at only thirteen years old) fell for the handsome prince. The two began exchanging letters, and in the summer of 1946 he asked for Princess Elizabeth's hand in marriage. Although Prince Philip was penniless, he was of royal blood and the proposal was accepted. He renounced his right to the Greek and Danish thrones, converted from the Orthodox Church to the Church of England, and became a British subject. The day before their wedding, King George VI bestowed the style His Royal Highness on Philip, and he was made a knight of the Order of the Garter. On the morning of the wedding, Philip was made the Duke of Edinburgh, Earl of Merioneth, and Baron Greenwich. These were the first of numerous titles he accrued.

Then in 1952, George VI died and Prince Philip's wife became Queen Elizabeth II. However irascible the prince may be in private (it is said that he has a temper shorter than an improvised explosive device), in public he knew his place. After the Queen was crowned in 1953, he made the pledge: 'I Philip, Duke of Edinburgh, do become your liege man of life and limb and of earthly worship; and faith and truth I will bear unto you, to live and die, against all manner of folks. So help me God.' He then had to retire from the Navy – a move which could not have been easy for the honoured officer – to become full-time royal consort, a role he has now fulfilled for over sixty years.

Over the past sixty years, a great deal has changed in Britain, but it was clear to Prince Philip that the royal family thrived on tradition. He dedicated himself to personifying the old values: patriotism, Anglicanism, hierarchy, pageantry, ceremony, and knowing which fork to use. He was irredeemably U – as opposed to non-U – as defined by Nancy Mitford in her 1954 essay 'The English Aristocracy.' The U here stands for 'upper class.' Those who are U say *napkin* rather than *serviette*, *lavatory* rather than *toilet*, and *vegetables* rather than *greens*.

It was also U to maintain wartime attitudes to foreigners. There were unreliable Italians, shifty Polish Jews, and weeping, romantic, fat Belgians. Military memos routinely referred to 'the Boche' and 'the Hun.' In Mitford's 1945 novel *The Pursuit of Love*, Uncle Matthew declares 'frogs are slightly better than Huns or wops, but abroad is unutterably bloody and foreigners are fiends.' Even Ian Fleming's James Bond novels that began in 1953 are riddled with casual national stereotypes and racial generalisations.

Such attitudes were commonplace. While others have become politically correct, Prince Philip has stuck to his guns. The prince does not do irony. He has no time for wordplay. His is the form of humour that identifies specific characteristics, exaggerates them, and then mocks them. He doesn't mean anything by it – Prince Philip comes from a generation that genuinely believes Johnny Foreigner quite likes being teased by us. The press may howl about his 'gaffes' – calling the Chinese 'slitty-eyed,' the Hungarians pot-bellied and the Aborigines spearchucker – but few take offence. Many of the old-school congratulate him for being 'forthright' and 'apologetic,' while those of a left-wing persuasion have long realised that such remarks are only made to get their dander up. He is like an aged uncle who likes to get a rise from the younger generation but, deep down, means no harm.

His humour comes from the ward room, when

Britain was at the height of empire. Most people from that era are now gone; those that remain have adapted to modern sensibilities. Prince Philip is unique in having survived with his seeming insensitivity intact, and he occupies a position in public life where he feels no need to button his lip. He is, quite simply, the upholder of an older humorous tradition, a living joke museum.

What's more, most of his witticisms are not delivered off the cuff. He puts a lot of work into what he has to say. And much of what he says is not without foundation. He often gives voice to what other people think, but are too afraid to express – in public, at least.

While some people do not find the prince's jokes amusing in themselves, they have stood the test of time. The rest of the royal family may clamour to update itself, but by cleaving to this ancient, creaking form of humour, Prince Philip has cemented his status as a king of comedy. If other people are not amused, he could not care less. As *The Times* put it on the event of his ninetieth birthday: 'The Duke of Edinburgh is a monument to a vanishing form of humour. We should celebrate him while we still can.'

The prince passed away on 9 April 2021 in the presence of his family.

In a heartfelt statement, Prince Harry recalled his grandfather with a beer in hand, 'master of the barbecue, legend of banter, and cheeky right 'til the end.'